The Political System of the Islamic Republic of Iran

The Political System of the Islamic Republic of Iran

M. Mahmood

Publications

KALPAZ PUBLICATIONS
DELHI - 110052

The Political System of the Islamic Republic of Iran

ISBN: 81-7835-520-5

Published in 2006 in India by
Kalpaz Publications
C-30, Satyawati Nagar, Delhi-110052
E-mail : kalpaz@hotmail.com

Laser Typesetting at: Tact Computer Graphics, Delhi
Printed at: Salasar Imaging System, Delhi

Contents

Preface 9

1. Iran between the Two Revolutions 1900-1979 13

The Constitutional Era. The Dictatorship of Reza Khan. The Reign of Muhammad Reza. The Revolution of 1979. The Making of the Islamic Republic. Consolidation of the Clerical Regime.

2. The Making of the Guardian Class 31

The Origin of Twelver Shiism. Shiism as State Religion in Iran. *Ijtihad, Mujtahid* and *Marja'iyyat*. The Political Role of the Iranian Mujtahids.

3. The Political Charter of Radical Shiism 49

Constitutionalism in the Islamic World. The Liberal Constitution and the Clerical Constitution. Authority and Legitimacy in the Islamic Republic.

4. The Guardianship of the Jurisconsult 59

The Leader at the Core. The Choice of the Leader. The Totalitarian Scope of Leader's Authority.

5. The Islamic Consultative Assembly 67

Parliamentary Elections. The Speaker of the Assembly. Parliamentary Standing Commissions. Parliamentary Procedure. The Role of Parliament. The Guardian Council. The Board for the Identification of the Expediency of the System. Popular Referendums. Local Consultative Councils.

6. The President of the Republic 81

The Mode of Presidential Election. The Role of the Executive President. The Presidential Cabinet. The National Security Council. The Armed Forces.

7. The Judicial Power 89

Islamization of the Judiciary. The President of the Judicial Power. The National Supreme Court. The Revolutionary Courts. The Ministry of Justice. The State Investigation Organization.

8. Political Parties in Iran 97

The Origins of Political Parties. Political Parties since 1979.

9. Iran in World Affairs 103

The Origins of Iranian Foreign Policy. Foreign Policy of the Pahlavi Regime. Foreign Relations of the Islamic Republic.

Conclusion 117

Appendix A: The Constitution of the Islamic Republic. 121

Appendix B: The Last Testament of Imam Khomeini. 189

Selected Bibliography 255

Index 263

Preface

Iran is an ancient civilization that has had a continuous existence for more than 3000 years. She is renowned for having made great contributions to art, science, literature, architecture, ethics, philosophy and religion. Her imprint on government and politics appears to be less significant because of the deeply entrenched tradition of despotism throughout.

Towards the end of the nineteenth century, however, under the impact of liberal ideas from the West, the Iranian intelligentsia launched a constitutional movement which culminated in the establishment of a constitutional regime in 1906. But the Constitutional Revolution came to an end by 1910 as conditions necessary for the success of constitutionalism and democracy were nonexistent in Iran of that time. The Qajars were eventually replaced by the Pahlavis who turned out to be greater despots. They asserted their kinship with the ancient Achaemenids and Sassanids, prescribed an Aryan identity and culture for the Iranians and ruled without restraints. The latter Pahlavi had allied himself with the mightiest power on earth against his own people but could not prevent them from rising in revolt against him and overthrowing his atrocious regime. The Revolution of 1979 did not usher in an era of freedom and democracy, again because of certain inherent flaws in Iranian society and politics, but culminated in yet another form of dictatorship. Thus Iran is akin to many developing countries which suffer from a crisis of authority and legitimacy and political stagnation. That does not, however, detract from the quest for understanding Iranian political institutions in their social and cultural context. This book is, therefore, designed to explain rather than to justify or denounce the present regime.

The book starts with an overview of the principal developments in Iran during 1900-1979 to set the stage for the onset of the revolution in 1979 and the emergence of the Islamic Republic. Chapter 2 then traces the origins and development through centuries of the guardian class of *Ithna Ashari* (twelver) mujtahids in Shiite Iran. By the force of circumstances, this guardian class which formerly exercised the guardianship of the community of the twelvers in religious and social affairs became politicized during the twentieth century and now forms the nucleus of the political system of Iran and the leading and guiding force of its society. Thereafter, Chapter 3 introduces the Constitution of the Islamic Republic which is truly the political charter of the Imamist system of government and reflects the political ideas and ideals of radical Shiism. This constitution is contrasted with the earlier liberal constitution to bring into bold relief the latter's authoritarian and totalitarian character. It is followed by Chapter 4 which analyzes the fundamental radical Shiite principle of *Vilayat-i-faqih* (the guardianship of the jurisconsult) and the attendant leadership structures. The rest of the book details the organization, inter-relationship and functioning of the three powers of government namely the legislative, the executive and the judicial and the associated auxiliaries of clerical hegemony. Chapter 8 is devoted to a survey of the development and decay of political parties in Iran since the nineteenth century to bring into focus the curious phenomenon of non-party government despite the proliferation of *licensed* pro-regime parties and groups. Finally, Iran's foreign policy during the Pahlavi and clerical eras has briefly been introduced. In the end, the text of the Constitution of 1979 and the *Last Testament* of Imam Khomeini have been added as appendices.

The financial assistance received from the Indian Council of Social Science Research, New Delhi, during 1994 which facilitated the completion of this work is gratefully acknowledged.

M. Mahmood
Department of Political Science
Aligarh Muslim University
Aligarh 202 002, India

1

Iran Between the Two Revolutions 1900-1979

The political history of Iran from 1900 to 1979 invariably displays two persistent features: (1) the quest for constitutionalism and democracy as against despotism and autocracy; and (2) the quest for modernization and development to deliver the Iranian masses from abject poverty and destitution. These aspirations were difficult to realize because of the deep-rooted virtues of selfishness, opportunism and authoritarianism. So Iran since 1900 has been ruled by the arbitrary will of persons and factions rather than in accordance with constitutional principles and procedures. The Constitutional Revolution of 1906 utterly failed to achieve its objectives because domestic feudalism and foreign powers interested in Iran made a common cause against constitutional government. This period is marked by three major events, each of which became a turning point in Iranian politics and, therefore, deserves a brief mention:

1. The Constitutional Revolution, 1905-1911;
2. The nationalization of the Iranian oil industry by the government of the National Front led by

Muhammad Musaddeq in 1951 and latter's dismissal through a CIA-sponsored *coup d' etat* in 1953; and

3. The popular revolution of 1979 which overthrew the Pahlavi monarchy.[1]

The Constitutional Era

Iran has had a persistent tradition of authoritarian rule over the past 3000 years. It was only during the latter half of the nineteenth century that the educated Iranians became familiar with Western ideals of liberalism, nationalism, constitutionalism and democracy. Some factors that contributed to the political awakening of Iranians were the spread of the modern system of education; the deputation of Iranian students to European countries for higher education; circulation of modern-style newspapers and periodicals; the influence of Iranian nationals living abroad; and the exemplary work done by European missionaries and experts deployed in Iran. Towards the close of the nineteenth century the corrupt and oppressive rule of the profligate Qajars had antagonized the three leading strata of the Iranian society of the time – the intellectuals, the mujtahids and the *bazaaris* (merchants). The intellectuals were motivated by the desire for reform and progress; the theologians wanted justice and freedom from foreign encroachments; and the *bazaaris* were extremely aggrieved by excessive and unjust taxation which crippled their business and commerce. This coalition of the three strata of the Iranian society was instrumental in the formation of a network of secret *anjumans* (associations) throughout the country to mobilize the public against arbitrary rule and in favour of agitation for rule of law and constitutional government.

Their demands were summed up in two points: that the king should grant a constitution (*mashrutah*) which regulated the organization and work of the government and that he should convene a national assembly to give expression to the will of the people. Early in 1906 a crowd of some 12000 constitutionalists assembled in Tehran by agitating over a few weeks forced the old and ailing king Muzaffaruddin Shah to submit to the wishes of his subjects. He promised to enact a constitution and convene a national assembly.

The first ever Constitution or the Fundamental Law of Iran was drafted by royal advisers and promulgated by a royal proclamation on 20 December 1906. Monarchy became constitutional and subservient to the will of the national assembly; the ministers of the crown became accountable to parliament; and the main demand of the constitutionalists that the power of the king in such matters as granting of concessions, monopolies and licences to foreigners, contracting of foreign loans and appropriation of money from the public exchequer should have prior parliamentary approval, was conceded under Articles 22-26 of the constitution.

The maiden *Majlis-i-Shura-i-Milli* (National Consultative Assembly), elected on a royal proclamation, was, however, not satisfied by the text of the constitution as drafted by the agents of the crown and demanded certain additions. Without waiting for royal response the parliamentarians themselves undertook the drafting of a Supplement to the Fundamental Law of 1906 which was readily signed by the king and promulgated in 1907. The Supplement, among other things, added four novel features to the Constitution: *First*, *Ithna Ashari* (twelver) Shiism was declared to be the state religion but at the same time all Iranians irrespective of their religion were guaranteed equal status and equal rights; *second*, as an important concession to the moderate mujtahids, who had supported the constitutional movement and were of the opinion that constitutional government should be in accordance with Islamic principles, it was provided that the National Consultative Assembly shall coopt a panel of five mujtahids of eminence who will certify the conformity of every parliamentary legislation with the Islamic *shariat*. (This provision was, however, never implemented); *third*, following Locke and Montesquieu, it was provided that the legislative, executive and judicial powers of government shall be kept separate, as their concentration in one person or body of persons was inimical to liberty and responsibility; and *finally*, a constitutional guarantee of civil liberties and certain individual fundamental rights was incorporated.

The first *Majlis* (National Consultative Assembly) was convened in Tehran on 7 October 1906 and Muzaffaruddin Shah died on 30 December 1907. He was succeeded by Muhammad Ali Shah, a staunch opponent of constitutionalism and a despot to the core. On 23 June 1908 he staged his infamous *coup d' etat* against the Majlis with the covert support of the Russian legation in Tehran and contingents drawn from the Russian-trained Cossaq Brigade at Tabrez. He then mercilessly bombarded the building of Majlis located in Baharistan area of Tehran, killing many liberal parliamentarians, and imposed martial law in the capital. Hearing the news of this barbaric action, the people of Tabrez rose in revolt against the king and took control of their city. Then in June 1909, Ali Quli Khan, a warlord of the Bakhtiari tribe, assembled a big force of pro-parliamentarians and began his march towards Tehran to restore the constitutional regime. On 12 July he stormed Tehran and on 16 July Muhammad Ali Shah took asylum in the Russian legation and later migrated to Russia. The restored Majlis then deposed him and put his minor son Ahmad Shah on the throne. The restored Majlis fell victim to factional fights and on 24 December 1911 a group of parliamentarians forcibly declared the closure of the Majlis and locked its doors. That marked the end of the constitutional era. Until the outbreak of World War I Iran was ruled by a coterie of nobles acting under Russian influence. The war years wrought utter devastation in Iran and the days of the old regime were numbered.

The constitutional regime appears to have failed because conditions necessary for the success of constitutionalism and democracy did not exist at the time. Some reasons for this failure were: (1) that the constitutionalist party lacked a central organization guided by a central leadership; they were a house divided among themselves; (2) the majority of the people were excluded from the constitutional movement because of their abject poverty and ignorance and thus the movement lacked a popular base; (3) the movement lacked a consensus on its ultimate goal: the intelligentsia desired a secular and liberal-democratic constitution; the moderate mujtahids were willing to accept a constitution that was compatible with the Islamic religion; and the orthodox mujtahids declared the very idea of a constitution as heresy and would agree to nothing short of a theocracy. Finally, both the great powers–Russia and Britain–which had carved out their spheres of influence in Iran were ill-disposed towards constitutionalism because their interests were presumably served better by an autocratic rather than a constitutional regime.

The Dictatorship of Reza Khan, 1921-41

By the time the third Majlis was convened on 7 December 1914, Iran was in utter chaos. The events of 1908-1909 had a devastating impact on the morale of the government and administration. The World War brought in its wake economic dislocation, social unrest and political uncertainty. Added to these was the indifferent attitude of the young and inexperienced constitutional monarch who appeared to be interested least in matters of state. In 1919 the Majlis rejected the draft Anglo-Iranian agreement proposed by Britain offering a package of financial and military assistance from Britain to Iran to overcome her national crisis on the ground that it was contrary to national sovereignty. In retaliation, the British government withdrew the British financial and military advisers from Iran. It was in this state of affairs in 1921 that one Ziauddin Tabatabai, an Iranian journalist with pro-British sympathies, is reported to have approached Reza Khan, then commander of the Cossaq Brigade in Tabrez (formed in 1878 with Russian instructors and training), to play a liberating role by overthrowing the decrepit government in Tehran. Reza Khan then marched to Tehran with some 3000 of his Cossaq troops. At the outskirts of Tehran he was repulsed by the royal troops but later, it is alleged, with the covert support extended by General Edmond Iron Side, the commander of the British troops stationed in Tehran, he was able to storm and capture Tehran. He then forced the formation of a government with Tabatabai as prime minister and himself as minister of war and the commander-in-chief of the armed forces. In this capacity he first unified the fragmented armed forces under his personal command, then on 28 October 1923 got himself appointed as prime minister. Disgusted with this nasty turn of events the young Shah left for Paris, never to come back to Iran (he died there in 1930).

Meanwhile, a section of military men began demanding removal of the king for long absence and declaration of Iran as a republic. Reza Khan too appeared to be favourable to the idea of a republic on the Turkish model. But the people would not let go their king. So they came out on the streets against the heresy of the republic. Sensing the mood of the public the Majlis rejected the idea of republic and inspired by the British, as it is alleged, amended the constitution to extinguish the Qajar dynasty and confer the crown of Iran on Reza Khan and his descendents in perpetuity. On 25 April 1926 Reza Khan crowned himself as Reza Shah Pahlavi.

On becoming king, Reza Khan, an unlettered crude military man, showed scant respect to the constitution and constitutional procedures. He banned all political parties and political activities, nullified civil liberties, made a mockery of parliamentary elections and handpicked his prime ministers and ministers arbitrarily to the exclusion of parliament. He soon earned notoriety for his atrocities, offending the religious sentiments of the people, persecuting the religious class, appropriating lands unjustly, awarding harsh punishments for petty offences, dismissing public servants people whimsically, and executing people wantonly.

Yet Reza Khan is also commended for having suppressed the tribal revolts, restoring the authority of the center over the whole of Iran, building a strong national army, expanding the system of public education, creating modern universities and colleges, and building modern roads, railways and hospitals. He banned traditional dress, prescribed European wear, abolished women's veil, banned *mut'a* (temporary marriage for pleasure allowed by the *Ithna Ashari* jurists), eliminated religious courts, and asserted his country's Aryan identity and culture. Moreover, he was a nationalist at heart: He abrogated all treaties which were derogatory to Iran's national honour and sovereignty. On 26 November 1932 he took the bold step of cancelling the oil concession originally granted in 1901 to a British national named William d' Arcy for a term of sixty years in lieu of a paltry royalty; (the concession was later taken over by the Anglo-Persian Oil Company floated by d' Arcy in 1909 and in 1914 the British Government acquired a controlling share in this company). But under pressure from the British Government Reza Khan retreated and on 29 May 1933 renewed the concession for yet another sixty years in lieu of a slightly higher royalty.

When World War II broke out the British suspected Reza Khan of making secret approaches to Nazi Germany. So they forced him to abdicate in favour of his minor son Muhammad Reza and exiled him to South Africa where he died later.

Reza Khan till this day has been a controversial person. While the royalist tribe eulogizes him as a great nation-builder and modernizer the clerical tribe denounces him as a vain tyrant, son of a stable boy (*bachcha-i-mehtar*) and an opium-eater (*taryaki*).

The Reign of Muhammad Reza, 1941-78

With Reza Khan in exile and his son on the throne the Iranians were relieved of a harsh dictatorship. Political freedom was restored and the Majlis was elected anew. Majlis once again became a forum for the expression of public opinion. But this proved to be a transient phase.

Ever since Reza Khan renewed the oil concession to the British in 1933 the Iranian nationalists had been complaining that the exchequer was losing an estimated sixteen billion Rials per annum on account of low royalty fixed in 1933. In 1951 the matter was debated hotly in the Majlis. As a panacea for all ills, a coalition of liberal nationalists and moderate mujtahids in the Majlis succeeded in March to push through a bill to nationalize the Iranian oil industry. In May the National Front (which had a majority in the Majlis) elected the firebrand nationalist Dr. Muhammad Musaddeq as its leader who was then appointed as prime minister by the king. The National Front then directed him to implement the oil nationalization bill. But the King refused to sign the bill into law and finding himself powerless before his parliament fled the country. The British and Americans would not countenance this state of affairs. So in 1953 the Central Intelligence Agency (CIA) of the USA got the Musaddeq government toppled through a military *coup d' etat*. Muhammad Reza was put back on the throne and he became an agent of Anglo-American interests. Constitutional monarchy was once again converted into a despotic monarchy. Following an attempt on his life in 1954 he became fearful of his people, isolated himself from them, took all powers in his own hands and decided to rule by an iron hand. With a view to uniformizing political life and imposing peace and order he abolished the multiparty system and floated an American-style two-party system. Next, to gain popular support he launched the so-called "White Revolution" on 26 January 1963 aiming at sweeping land reforms and socio-economic transformation in the countryside. By acquiring the estates of big landlords and redistributing the land among the landless he aimed at reducing the potential of agrarian unrest, weakening the hold of the *khans* (landlords) and undermining the power of tribal chiefs.

One fall out of these reforms was that many mujtahids were divested of the control of large *waqf* (Muslim endowment) properties under their management whose income sustained them and their students in the seminaries run by them. The king had hit hard at the belly of the mujtahids so they turned against him. In June 1963 the clergy organized a massive public demonstration against king's policies in the holy city of Qum. This demonstration was brutally suppressed by the royal police. After this event student and youth organizations went under ground to prepare for a future guerilla warfare against the regime and the clergy were launched on a course of indoctrination and mobilization of the masses against royal tyranny. Among those arrested for leading anti-Shah demonstration in Qum was Ayatullah Ruhullah Musavi al-Khomeini who was then principal of the Faiziyya Seminary at Qum. For speaking against the king he was exiled first to Turkey and then from there to Iraq in 1964. Forced by Iraqi government to leave the country he sought political asylum in France in 1978 and settled in a Paris suburb from where he guided and directed the revolutionary struggle in Iran during 1978-79.

Following the upheaval of 1963 the king did nothing to assuage the feelings of his people. He was too much confident of his own power and of the American support to deal with his domestic opposition. Whatever he did thereafter added fuel to fire and further antagonized the people against him. In 1971 he spent billions on the vainglorious celebration of the 2,500 year of the Pahlavi monarchy. In 1972 he signed a capitulations agreement with the American government granting diplomatic immunity to American experts and advisers deployed in Iran. In 1975 he disbanded the official two-party system and created a single state party named *Rastakhiz*

[Resurgence] membership of which was made compulsory for all Iranians. Further, in his last years American advisers were employed in large numbers that gave the impression of Iran becoming an American protectorate.

The Revolution of 1979

The seeds of the revolution of 1979 lay in the events and developments of the period 1953-78. Main causes of this revolutionary upheaval have been identified as (1) the oppressive and repressive character of the regime which had blocked all avenues of political expression and participation, banned political dissent and opposition and converted Iran into a police-state; (2) growing socio-economic disparities and the widening gap between the rich and poor; (3) the pseudo or erring modernization policies which led to mass unemployment and misery; (4) foreign and defence policies of the regime were perceived to be anti-national and offended the sentiments of the people; and finally, the regime's denigration of the religious class and secularization policies. All these and other causes cumulatively eroded the authority and legitimacy of the regime. Popular anger was intensifying day by day. A provocative article published in a Tehran daily on 7 January 1978 which defamed the mujtahids in general and attacked Khomeini in particular as a pervert and a foreign agent of British Indian origin (his family had migrated from Lucknow city of north India to Iran during the nineteenth century), ignited the revolt. To protest against this his followers staged massive demonstrations in Qum and Tabrez. Some thirty demonstrators were killed in police firings that day.

That started a chain reaction throughout the country. The underground guerilla groups sprang to action against government forces. The people everywhere struck work and organized rallies and protest marches. Then refinery workers at Abadan struck work and brought oil production to a halt. The regime tried to put down the revolt with a heavy hand. Some 60,000 people were killed; more than one lac maimed or disabled, and millions of dollar worth property destroyed. As advised by the Americans, the king went into exile on 11 January 1979; the American advisers left Tehran on 1 February 1979; and the Pahlavi regime collapsed midnight of 10-11 February 1979.

Although the revolt of 1979 was a popular democratic revolt jointly waged by the masses, the mujtahids, the democratic forces and the guerilla fighters of both left and right the mujtahids christened it as "the Islamic Revolution" because under the guidance and leadership of Ayatullah Khomeini the mujtahids and their followers were in the forefront of the uprising. During the days of upheavals they formed revolutionary committees everywhere, created parallel administrative agencies, maintained the essential services, and ensured the supply of basic necessities to the people so when the end of the Pahlavi regime came the clergy instantly took over the machinery of the state and established their rule.

The Making of the Islamic Republic

During the uprising Revolutionary Committees were formed by the clergy to deal with their opponents and afterwards Revolutionary Courts were established and Revolutionary Prosecutors appointed to apprehend, prosecute and punish the functionaries of the former regime found guilty of committing atrocities against the people. Soon after the overthrow of the Pahlavi regime the leader of the revolution Ayatullah Khomeini appointed a Revolutionary Council, composed of the leading mujtahids close to him, as an interim supreme policy-making authority. Then on 11 February 1979 he appointed a Provisional Government with Mahdi Bazargan, an engineer educated in France, as prime minister and composed of both the mujtahids and leading liberal intellectuals who had fought against the old regime. Then on 29 March 1979 a national referendum was held to enable the people to choose between monarchy and an Islamic republic. An overwhelming majority voted in favour of an Islamic replublic.

Meanwhile, Prime Minister Bazargan with his team had prepared a draft of a French-style democratic constitution incorporating Islamic principles of government as well. He visualized Iran as an "Islamic Democratic Republic". Bazargan proposed to Khomeini that a Constituent Assembly be elected to consider and approve the draft. Khomeini disapproved the idea of convening a constituent assembly as it would be cumbersome and time-consuming. He instead proposed the election of an Assembly of Experts to consider and adopt a final draft. Ultimately Khomeini's will prevailed. The constitutional draft was published on 18 June 1979; a 73-member Assembly of Experts was elected on 3 August 1979 with mujtahids forming a clear majority. The Assembly elected Ayatullah Muhammad Husain Beheshti, a leading mujtahid and a right-hand man of Khomeini, as its Chairman. After due deliberations the Assembly rejected Bazargan's idea of an Islamic *democratic* government and instead incorporated Khomeini's concept of *Vilayat-i-faqih* (guardianship of the jurisconsult) as the core concept of the new constitution. The Assembly finally approved the draft on 15 November 1979. It was then approved by the people by an overwhelming majority in a national referendum held on 2-3 December 1979.

In accordance with Articles 5 and Articles 107-112 of the Constitution, Ayatullah Khomeini was coopted by the consensus of the community as the *Valiyy-i-faqih* (designated as the Leader of the Islamic Revolution and the Custodian of the Affairs of the Muslims of the World) for life. Bazargan resigned as prime minister of the Provisional Government on 5 November 1979. The first election of the President of the Republic was held in January 1980. The Revolutionary Council was dissolved on 18 July 1980. Soon afterwards the newly elected President of the Republic appointed the first regular cabinet. The first elections to the *Majlis-i-Shura-i-Islami* (the Islamic Consultative Assembly) took place in March and May 1980.

As Khomeini was of advanced age and frail health, the need of choosing his successor in advance was felt. For this purpose a *Majlis-i-Khobregan-i-Rahbari* (Assembly of Experts on Leadership) was elected in 1982 by an electorate composed of the members of the clerical class. This body failed to arrive at a consensus over the question of the Leader's successor. The matter was referred to Khomeini who then nominated his closest disciple and an illustrious scholar Ayatullah Hussein Ali Muntazeri as his successor. His appointment was not countenanced by intriguers who themselves aspired to succeed the Leader. As a result, the old man's ears were consistently fed against Muntazeri. Ultimately Khomeini was turned against him and a few months before his death he asked Muntazeri to resign as his successor which he did.

After Khomeini's death on 3 June 1989, Hojjatul Islam Sayyid Ali Khamenei (then President of the Republic) was elected as the Leader of the Islamic Revolution and his rival Hojjatul Islam Akbar Hashemi Rafsanjani (then speaker of the Islamic Consultative Assembly) was elected as the President of the Republic. That settled the question of succession.

Consolidation of the Clerical Regime

In its early days the revolutionary regime was beset by very many problems and its existence was threatened by many internal and external enemies. Its eventual consolidation and confirmation can be attributed to three national catastrophes which occurred one after another and each rallied the people behind the regime:

1. The seizure of the American embassy in Tehran on 4 November 1979 by a group of radical students calling themselves "The Followers of the Line of the Imam" and holding of some 65 members of the embassy staff as hostages until 20 January 1981. They demanded that the USA repatriate the Shah of Iran who had taken refuge in America.
2. The tragic bombing on 28 June 1981 by some foreign-inspired terrorist group of the headquarters of the ruling Islamic Republican Party (*Hizb-i-Jumhuriyy-i-Islami*) in Tehran which killed some 70 top-ranking leaders of the regime assembled there. Yet another terroristic bombing of the office premises of the prime minister on 30 August 1981 killed the incumbent President Muhammad Ali Rejai and the incumbent Prime Minister Javad Bahonar; and
3. The treacherous Iraqi invasion of Iran on 22 September 1980 which started the long-drawn Iraq-Iran War ending on 20 August 1988.

The first catastrophe immobilized the American embassy (dubbed by the revolutionaries as a *lana-i-*

jasoosi (espionage den) and prevented it from engineering a *coup d' etat* against the revolutionary regime in the style of one staged in 1953. Incidentally, this episode also caused the liberal collaborators of the mujtahids to part their company, as Prime Minister Bazargan protested against this brazen violation of international law on 4 November and demanded an immediate end of the siege. Next day he and his liberal colleagues resigned from the Provisional Government. Bazargan then left Iran in disgust and lived in Paris till his death in 1995.

The resignation of the Provisional Government over hostage-taking led to an immediate split between the liberals and the conservative majority in the regime. Skirmishes took place between the supporters of President Abol Hasan Bani Sadr and the cadres of the Islamic Republican Party in the streets of Tehran. Bani Sadr was then accused of treachery and treason, impeached by the Majlis on 21 June 1981 and dimissed from his office by the Leader Ayatullah Khomeini in July. He then fled Iran along with Masud Rajavi, the leader of the Mujahideen-i-Khalq, and took refuge in France. Thereafter the regime launched an all-out offensive against all the nationalist, liberal-democratic and Marxist parties and groups. A blanket ban was imposed on the National Front, the National Freedom Movement and the Tudeh Party. The regime thus eliminated all its potential political rivals from the scene.

The second catastrophe prodded the regime to exterminate all guerilla groups and armed bands of both the left and right particularly the *Fidayeen-i-Khalq* (an offshoot of the Tudeh Party) and the *Mojahideen-i-Khalq* (an offshoot of the National Freedom Movement). Thus the regime became safe from domestic terrorism.

The third and the most devastating catastrophe was the Iraq's wanton aggression against Iran. The war rekindled the national feeling among the Iranian masses and they rallied behind the regime and made exemplary sacrifices in the Defence of their motherland.

Having thus weathered all stresses and strains the regime demonstrated its ability to survive and stand on its own feet.

Reference

1. For details see E.G. Browne, *The Persian Revolution* 1905-1909 (Cambridge:Cambridge University Press,1911); Ervand Abrahamian, *Iran between the Two Revolutions:* James A. Bill and W.R. Louis, eds., *Musaddeq, Iranian Nationalism and Oil;* Huma Katouzian, *Musaddeq and the Struggle for Power in Iran;* and Mansur Farhang, "How the Clergy Gained Power in Iran," in *The Islamic Impulse,* ed. by B.F. Stowasser (London: Croom Helm, 1987).

2

The Making of the Guardian Class

The political system of the Islamic Republic is hinged on the cardinal principle of *vilayat-i-faqih* (the guardianship of the jurisconsult). The *valiyy-i-faqih* or the guardian jurisconsult (designated as the Leader of the Islamic Revolution and the Custodian of the Affairs of the Muslims of the World) is drawn from among the guardian class of *Ithna Ashari* mujtahids (the twelver theologian-jurists). This guardian class claims to be the inheritor of the mantle of the twelve Imams of the Shiite community and repository of their absolute authority in both spiritual and temporal matters. As such they demand absolute loyalty and total obedience from the Imamist community. This guardian class which in the past played a leading and guiding role in religious and charitable matters only became during the twentieth century by the force of circumstances politicized and claimed to exercise the political and governmental leadership of the community as well. In the post-revolutionary Iran this class forms the nucleus of its political system and the leading and guiding force of its society. This direct assumption of political leadership by a class of religious scholars and jurists is a unique phenomenon in the entire history of the Islamic world since the splitting of the secular and religious leadership of the Islamic community in 661 AD. The rise of the twelver mujtahids as a corporate force should be seen as a unique phenomenon associated with the unique history, politics, society and culture of Iran since 1500 AD.

The Origin of Twelver Shiism

The Arabic term *shi'a* means a faction or party. Initially persons who supported Ali Ibn Abi Talib, the fourth legitimate successor of Prophet Muhammad and the Commander of the Faithful, in his campaign against Amir Mu'awiyya, the governor of the Syrian Province who had declared his independence of the centre. In this power struggle the partisans of Ali came to be known as *Shii* or Shiites in due course Shiism evolved as a dissenting and distinct sect within the mainstream Islam. Some people assert that twelver Shiism is a self-contained religion parallel to the mainstream Islam with its separatist doctrines, its own books of traditions, its own school of jurisprudence and its own peculiar rites and rituals. Shiism in all its variety is founded on the core doctrine of divine and hereditary *imamat* (spiritual and temporal leadership of the community after the Prophet) as opposed to the classical Sunnite doctrine of *khilafat* (vicegerency of the Prophet in spiritual and temporal affairs of the community) which is popular rather than divinely ordained and elective rather than hereditary. Subsequently the doctrine of *Imamat* gave birth to a number of Shiite subsects such as the Zaidiyya, Sab'iyya, Ismailiyya and the Ithna Ashariyya (twelvers). The latter became the dominant and more numerous sect with its followers spread in Iran, Iraq, Lebanon, Bahrain and the countries of the Indian subcontinent. Our discussion of the genesis and growth of the guardian class of twelver mujtahids first as religious leaders and then as political leaders as well hinges on an exposition of the peculiar doctrines of this twelver sect.

The first core belief of Shiism is the belief in the divine and hereditary nature of *imamat*. The Shiites contend that the authority to lead the believers after him was transferred by the Prophet Muhammad to his cousin and son-in-law Ali Ibn Abi Talib and his male descendants. Designated as *imams* (leaders and guides) they are believed to have divine sanctity, infallibility and immunity from sinful acts. Since their authority is believed to have been delegated by the Prophet and the God Almighty it is held to be divine and sacred, eternal and immutable and inviolable.[2]

The second core belief of the twelvers is the belief in the *ghaibat* (disappearance or occultation) of the twelfth and last Imam. This doctrine of occulatation is understood to have been formulated by one Abu Sahl Ali bin Ismail, a medieval Shiite scholar of Iranian descent, to ensure the survival and guide the conduct of a vulnerable minority sect amidst a hostile Sunnite majority. According to this doctrine, the cycle of the twelve divinely ordained Imams came to an end in 873/4 AD when Muhammad al-Mahdi, the infant son and successor of the eleventh Imam, Hasan al-Askari, went into occultation till such time as the world becomes full of injustice to the brim. He will then reappear to establish rule of justice upon earth. After the belief in God and the Prophet every twelver is enjoined to believe in the eternal presence and the expected return of Mahdi the Hidden Imam and to render him total loyalty and obedience.[3]

This esoteric doctrine had two important implications for the Shiite community and guides their conduct at all times and in all places. First, in the absence of the legitimate authority of the Hidden Imam the faithful are free to acquiesce in and submit to the illegitimate authority of the temporal rulers for the time-being. But they can neither support them actively nor oppose them actively; they should simply remain calm and quiet and adopt a passive attitude. Second, for the sake of self-preservation and security amidst a hostile people the faithful are enjoined to practise *taqayyeh* (dissimulation) or practice of double morality and concealment of one's true identity, beliefs and actions while interacting with other communities.

Third fundamental belief of twelvers is the belief in *vilayat-i-amma* (general guardianship), that is, during the absence of the Hidden Imam the custodianship of the general affairs of the twelver community on his behalf truly and legitimately belongs to the twelver mujtahids who are the true delegates and legatees of the Hidden Imam. The background and the necessity of this doctrine lies in the fact that for about a century after the supposed disappearance of the last Imam, the twelvers conducted their affairs in accordance with the teachings and rulings of the Imams. But with the passage of time newer problems and situations arose and the necessity of deducing new rules from the established rules by the competent scholars and jurists for the benefit of laymen who were not well-versed in matters of religion and law was felt. This intellectual endeavour came to be known as *ijtihad* and its practitioners were designated as *mujtahid* (jurisconsults). The status and role of the *mujtahids* in the twelver community is based on the postulate that just as the Prophet Muhammad was an intermediary between God Almighty and the community of believers so were Prophet's successors (the twelve Imams) intermediaries between the Prophet and the community of the faithful and *ipso facto* the mujtahids are intermediaries between the holy Imams and the twelver community. The *ijtihadi* school also corroborates the doctrine of *ijtihad* by a decree stated to have been issued by the Hidden Imam from his occultation to his followers which ordained that "Concerning the new cases that arise, refer to the transmitters of our traditions, for they are my *hujja* (proof) unto you just as I am God's *hujja* (proof) unto them."[4]

This doctrine of the custodianship of the jurisconsults in religious, charitable and social affairs of the twelver community became fully established by the middle of the nineteenth century. Regarded as the inheritors of the holy mission of the holy Imams the mujtahids are shown great reverence and they exert great moral influence upon their community. In course of time they assumed a corporate identity, developed a sort of informal hierarchical ranks among themselves and entrenched themselves in well-endowed seminaries at centres of learning.

The Chain of the Twelve Imams

Prophet Muhammad (died 630 AD)

1. Ali Ibn Abi Talib (d. 661 AD)
2. Al-Hasan (d. 669 AD)
3. Al-Husain (d. 680 AD)
4. Ali Ibn Husain Zainul Abedin (d. 714 AD)
5. Muhammad al-Baqar (d. 733 AD)
6. Jafar as-Sadiq (d. 765 AD)
7. Musa al-Kazim (d. 799 AD)
8. Ali ar-Raza (d. 818 AD)
9. Muhammad Jawad at-Taqi (d. 835 AD)
10. Ali an-Naqi (d. 868 AD)
11. Al-Hasan az-Zaki al-Askari (d. 874 AD)
12. Muhammad al-Mahdi (disappeared 874AD).

It was to a Grand Mujtahid of the twentieth century to extend the doctrine of the custodianship of the jurisconsult from the religious and social realm to the political realm by logical reasoning. He thus overturned the age-old twelver tradition of quietism, passivity and depoliticization and assigned the mujtahids of the time the primary duty of establishing and running Islamic government in their country. He thereby cancelled the necessity of waiting indefinitely for the return of the Hidden Imam to establish justice on earth. The mujtahids, being his legatees and counterparts, are equally competent to establish just rule here and now.

Shiism as State Religion in Iran

Shiism became the ascendant religion in Persia when Ismail Safavi,[5] a Turkoman chieftain of the Shiite creed, defeated his rival tribal chiefs and declared himself as king of Persia in 1501 with his capital at Ardbil. He then declared twelver Shiism as the state religion and ordered forcible conversion of the Sunnite majority to Shiism. Those who did not convert were either beheaded or banished. Historians point out that Ismail's motive in making Shiism the national religion of Persia was that he wanted to preserve the independence of his dominion against the mighty Ottoman Empire in the west, ruled by the Sunnite sultans. He was afraid that Persia might be absorbed in Turkey.

Ismail not only declared Shiism as the national religion of Iran but also created a religious department headed by a *Sadr* or *Mullabashi* (head priest) and staffed by twelver Mujtahids to administer religious affairs and oversee conversions. Thus was laid the foundation of an official clergy in Iran. ujtahids who did not join the state service were left to pursue their own ends.

Ijtihad, Mujtahid and *Marja'iyyat*

The twelver doctrines of *imamat, vilayat, ijtihad* and *marja'iyyat* are interrelated and interdependent concepts. The holy Imams are believed to have derived their authority from the Prophet Muhammad and the last (occulted) Imam in the chain of *imamat* is belived to have delegated his authority to the twelver mujtahids who are now the custodians of affairs of the twelver community on his behalf. The necessity of having a body of mujtahids in the community arises from the fact that not everybody in the community is competent to comprehend and apply the Imamite rules of law in his own discretion and judgment. So in matters of religion and law the lay and unlearned persons are bound to follow one of the mujtahids as their guide or source of reference or emulation. The theologian-jurist whose guidance is sought and whose advice is acted upon by the followers is called a mujtahid or *marja'* (source of reference and guidance). The laymen who follow a mujtahid are called *muqallid* (followers or adherents). Now it is an established rule of twelver jurisprudence that every twelver must either become a mujtahid or become a *muqallid* of one of mujtahids, that is, must adopt him as his *marja'* (source of reference and guidance).

This doctrine of the interposition of mujtahids between the twelve Imams and the twelver community was challenged by the so-called *Akhbari* (traditionalist) school of twelver jurisprudence who denied the necessity of any intermediation between the Imams and their followers and denounced the newly invented doctrine of *ijtihad* as being repugnant to the divinely ordained, inalienable and exclusive authority of the Imams. However, by the middle of the nineteenth century the radical *usuli* or *ijtihadi* school gained mass acceptance and the *Akhbaris* passed into obscurity.[6]

Ijtihad (literally means discovering something by diligence) has been defined in varying but overlapping terms as "The discovery and authoritative enunciation of fresh legal norms, based on a comprehensive knowledge of the *shariat* and traditions and arrived at by supreme effort and endeavour;" or as "The search for correct opinions on the basis of *usul* (general norms) and *ahkam* (particular ordinances);" or as "Expending one's utmost effort in the inquiry into legal questions admitting of only probable answers." In twelver jurisprudence the exercise of *ijtihad* is considered a *farz-i-kifaya* (a communal obligation which is deemed to have been discharged by all if fulfilled by a few of the community). So every twelver is in principle and in practice either a *mujtahid* or a *muqallid*. If he happens to be a *muqallid* (lay follower) he is at liberty to adopt any one of the *mujtahids* as his *marja'*; he can also change one *marja'* for another. He can also condult with more than one *marja'*. A mujtahid, on the other hand, is one who undergoes a definite course of training in religious and legal studies and after fulfilling certain conditions is acknowledged as a mujtahid. He is a scholar, a theologian, a jurist, an opinion-writer on legal matters (*mufti*) and a teacher and preacher, all at the same time.

In course of time the most learned and most eminent mujtahid or a number of mujtahids were given the honorific title of *Ayatullah* (Symbol of God). By the end of the nineteenth century their duties included the management of *awqaf* (religious endowments) and the guardianship and maintenance of minors, orphans, widows and destitutes.[7] They are entitled to collect the compulsory religious tithes from the faithful like *zakat, ushr, khomos* and the voluntary *sahm-i-imam*, other alms, and income derived from religious endowments and to spend the same for religious and charitable purposes like maintenance of mosques, seminaries and schools, orphanages and other charitable institutions.[8]

The informal clerical hierarchy that took shape during the nineteenth century and was further refined during the twentieth century is depicted below:

Clerical Hierarchy in Iran c. 2006

1. *Marja'-i-taqlid-i-kull* (universal source of reference and guidance) who carried the honorific title of *Ayatullah il uzma* (Greatest Symbol of God).

2. Other eminent *maraje'-i-taqlid* who may exist at any given time who also carry the honorific title of *Ayatullah il uzma* (Greatest Symbol of God) and a large number of them may exist at a given time.

3. Candidate Mujtahids who carry the honorific title of *hojjatul Islam wal Muslimeen* (proof of Islam and Muslims).

4. Junior Mujtahids who are freshly graduated from the seminaries of Qum, Mashhad and Najaf and carry the honorific title of *thiqatul Islam* (the trusted of Islam).

5. Akhunds or ordinary religious teachers and preachers who carry no honorific title and are the proletariat of the religious class.

The qualifications prescribed for becoming a mujtahid include first, adequate proficiency in Arabic language and literature; *second, perfect* knowledge of the holy Quran and the sayings of the holy Imams;

third, satisfactory expertise in twelver jurisprudence; and *fourth*, an aptitude for logical reasoning and deductive ability. A candidate is required to receive his religious education in one or more theological seminaries located at Qum and Mashhad in Iran and Najaf in Iraq. Besides, on completion of his studies he must obtain an *ijazeh* (testimonial) from one or more eminent professors at these seminaries testifying to his accomplishments and good conduct. *Finally*, he must gather around him a group of *muqallids* (followers) who acknowledge him as their *marja'* (source of reference or guidance).

The institution of *marja'iyyat* (elegibility to act as a source of reference or guidance) was established during the Safavid era. At any given time any number of eminent mujtahids may be acknowledged by the community as *maraje'-i-taqlid* (sources of reference and guidance). Moral and intellectual qualities required of a *marja'-i-taqlid* are maturity, intelligence, male gender, piety, integrity, righteousness and legitimate birth. There is no formal machinery or a set procedure for the appointment of a person as a *marja'-i-taqlid*. This status is not bestowed but informally acknowledged on the basis of universal consensus among the twelvers. Similarly, the practice of acknowledging one of the most senior, most senior, and most learned mujtahids of the Shiite world as the *marja'-i-taqlid-i-kull* (universal source of reference and guidance) also originated during the nineteenth century. This topmost rank among the twelver clergy has a striking resemblance with the position of the Pope of the Roman Catholic Church. The chain of the universal sources of reference that has existed since the nineteenth century is depicted below:

The Chain of Universal Sources of References

1. Al-Hajj Sheikh Muhammad Hasa Isfahani (died 1850)
2. Sheikh Muraza Ansari (d. 1864)
3. Mirza Hasan Shirazi (d. 1895)
4. Mulla Muhammad Kazim Khurasani (d. 1911)
5. Sayyid Muhammad Kazim Tabatabai (d. 1919)
6. Mirza Muhammad Taqi Haeri (d. 1920)
7. Sheikh Fazlulllah Isfahani (d. 1920; held the rankonly for four months)
8. Al-Hajj Sayyid Abul Hasan Musavi (d. 1946)
9. Sayyid Aqa Husain ibn Muhammad Tabatabai (d. 1947)
10. Al-Hajj Aqa Husain Brujerdi (d. 1961)
11. Ruhullah Musavi al-Khomeini (d. 1989)
12. Muhammad Ali Araki (d. 1994)
13. Muhammad Husain Shirazi (d. 2001)
14. Sayyid Ali Khamenei (1994)

The sources of the influence of the mujtahids in the post-Qajar Iran are as follows; *first*, the relative autonomy of the mujtahids from the political establishment; *second*, the institution of *marja'iyyat*; *third*, the rootedness of the mujtahids in the community since they originate from among the common people and work and live among them for life; *fourth*, besides performing religious services for the community they also perform certain essential social functions like guardianship and maintenance of the orphans, widows, destitutes and providing succor to the poor and needy; and *finally*, their relative financial independence as they derive their income from religious endowments placed under their management and from mandatory religious tithes and alms collected by them and spent it on a host of religious, educational, and charitable purposes in their discretion.

The Political Role of the Mujtahids, 1501-1953

Twelver political jurisprudence draws a clear line between *de jure* and *de facto* authority. *De jure* or legitimate authority is vested eternally in the immortal Hidden Imam and the *de facto* or existing authority of the temporal rulers of all times is but a usurpation of the authority of the Hidden Imam and by definition illegitimate. The twelvers are enjoined to render only passive obedience to temporal rulers or practise passive resistance if they like, but never, in principle, to justify or uphold their authority. During the Safavid era no conflict between the mujtahids and the state developed because the Safavids claimed to rule as the descendants of the holy Imams and also because they had coopted the mujtahids into the state establishment leaving them no room to resist or oppose the state. Similarly, mujtahids outside the state establishment were non-political and were confined to their religious and academic pursuits.[9]

However, if Safavids dealt with mujtahids on a footing of equality because they claimed to be the descendants of Ali their successors, the Qajars, had no such advantage and rather claimed to rule by the divine right and preferred for themselves the title of *zillullah* (Shadow of God). At the same time, they acknowledged the religious authority of the mujtahids, regarded them as the well-wishers of the state and used to seek their blessings. The mujtahids in return acknowledged the king as the defender of the faith and benefactor of the religious class. But with the decadence and degeneration of the Qajars during the nineteenth century this mutual understanding came to an end. Misrule, corruption, extravagance and plundering of public money, atrocities committed against the common people, and the infamous financial deals of the Qajars with foreigners for petty personal gains alienated the religious class from the state and put them on the path of opposition to tyranny and misrule and foreign encroachment.

Subsequently, the mujtahids launched a series of protest movements against such anti-national movements against such anti-national deals as the Reuter's concession (1872), the Tobacco monopoly (1890) and licence granted to a Belgian to run a lottery in Iran. The mujtahids declared both the use of tobacco and joining the lottery as *haraam* (religiously forbidden) and the people obeyed their injunction throughout the country. Ultimately, with the support of the people they succeeded in forcing the king to cancel all such nefarious deals.

A great event of the early twentieth century was the launching of the Constitutional Movement during 1905-06. The mujtahids were sharply divided among themselves on the issue of constitutionalism. While moderates like Sheikh Ismail Mahallati and Mirza Muhammad Husain Na'ini considered constitutional government as being nearest to Islamic government the extremists like Sheikh Faslullah Nuri were deadly opposed to constitutionalism and regarded it as heresy. They would agree to nothing but pure Islamic government. For instance, Sayyid Ali Sistani issued a *fatwa* (legal opinion) declaring that "Constitutionalism is infidelity and a constitutionalist is an infidel; his property is spoils and his blood worth shedding."[10] The moderate mujtahids joined the constitutional movement along with the intellectuals and the bazaaris and contributed to its success. The orthodox mujtahids kept away from it and sided with the anti-constitutionalists. The staunchest anti-constitutionalist of the time Sheikh Fazlullah Nuri was tried for treason and hanged in 1909.

In deference to the wishes of the moderate mujtahids who had sided with the constitutional movement the liberals inserted an article in the Constitutional Supplement of 1907 to the effect that the National Consultative Assembly may appoint a panel of five eminent mujtahids to review the compatibility of each legislation passed by the Assembly with the Islamic religion and to nullify it if found contrary to it. However, with the relapse of despotism like many other provisions this too was never acted upon.

Disgusted with Reza Khan's forcible assumption of the post of prime minister, king Ahmad Shah left in 1924 for Paris for a vacation, never to come back to Iran. Meanwhile, a section of the military who were impressed by the declaration of Turkey as a republic campaigned for the dismissal of the absent king and proclamation of Iran as a republic. Reza Khan too appeared to be sympathetic to this idea. But the conservative mujtahids regarded monarchy as sacrosanct and mobilized the ignorant masses against the republic. Street demonstrations were organized and some people even went to the Russian legation to seek its help against republicanism. Reza Khan felt disappointed and appeared to resign as prime minister. But then the British are believed to have converted him from republicanism to monarchism. It was proposed that Reza Khan himself should become the king of Iran. Thereupon a constitutional amendment was introduced in the Majlis whereby the Qajar dynasty was extinguished and the crown of Iran was conferred upon Reza Khan and his descendents for ever. Reza Khan then crowned himself as Reza Shah Pahlavi on 25 April 1926. [11]

The period of Reza Khan's dictatorship (1921-41) witnessed the transformation of Iran from a feudal agrarian and splintered country into a modern centralized nation-state. The religious class in the beginning took him as another national reformer the like of Mirza Muhammad Taqi Khan Amir-i-kabir. So they did not meddle in politics. Reza Khan too appeared to be deferent towards the religious class. But gradually as his policy of westernization of Iran unfolded he began to see the religious class as an obstacle in his way. He then began harassing and persecuting them. They suffered all sorts of indignity passively. Ayatullah Khomeini has recalled his experience of those days in these words: "Ever since Reza Khan came to power I saw that whatever was good to Islam was subjected to attack. In those days the *rowhaniyyat* (the religious class) was the bulwark against the tide of foreign influence. So they became a target of violent attacks. They were then harassed so much that we were forced to pass our time roaming about in the gardens of Qum from morning till evening."[12]

The dictatorship of Reza Khan came to an end in 1941 when Allied Powers forced him to abdicate in favour of his minor son for hobnobbing with Nazi Germany. The transitional period from 1941 to 1950 was marked by relaxation of dictatorship and resumption of political activities. In the beginning Muhammad Reza too like his father was deferent to the religious class. He also restored the exemption from compulsory military service to seminary students withdrawn by Reza Khan in 1938.[13] Relations between the clergy and the state then rested on mutual accommodation and non-interference in each other's sphere.

Then followed the tumultuous years of 1951-1953. The period became once again a turning-point in Iranian history. Musaddeq was toppled and Muhammad Reza was restored to the throne. Constitutional monarchy once again degenerated into absolute monarchy. The Shah, was launched on a course of domestic repression and alliance with foreign powers. With a view to undercutting his domestic opposition and enlarging his social base the Shah, under American inspiration, embarked on a programme of sweeping land reforms in the countryside (the so-called "White Revolution") which affected adversely the religious class. In the new policies and programmes the clergy saw an attempt to wipe out the religious class and undermine the traditional social order. The period of oppression and repression from 1953 to 1978 has been described by the clergy as 25 years of *ikhtenaq-i-mutlaq* (absolute choking). It was during this period that a quietist and non-political clergy became swiftly politicized and was launched on a radical course of anti-monarchism. It saw the monarchy as an enemy of the clergy and the people at large and therefore aimed at overthrowing it by revolutionary action.

The Vanguard of a Revolution, 1963-79

The developments that took place in Iran between the two revolutions in general and between 1953 to 1963 in particular made the clergy realize that the monarchical regime was not only despotic and tyrannical but was also out to destroy the religion, culture, traditions and customs of the country along with the religious class. The instinct of self-preservation, then, forced them to take to indoctrination and mobilization of the people against the unjust regime. Thus they became the revolutionary vanguard of the uprising of 1978-79, toppled the royal regime, created an Islamic Republic, adopted an Islamic Constitution and became the leading and guiding force of the Iranian state and society.

References

1. About the fundamentals of the Shiite religion as discussed by a leading *Ithna Ashari* mujtahid, see Sayyid Muhammad Husayn Tabatabai, *Shiite Islam,* translated from Farsi and edited with an introduction and notes by Sayyid Husain Nasr (London: Allen & Unwin, 1975); see also the article on "Ithna Ashariyya" in the *The Encyclopedia of Islam*, edited by H.A.R. Gibb.

2. This belief in the *vilayat* of Ali is affirmed in the *Ithna Ashari* form of *adzan* (call to prayers) which includes the recitation that "I testify that Ali is *vali-ul-lah"* [vicegerent of God]. Whether Ali was nominated by the Prophet Muhammad as his heir and successor for the leadership of the community is a matter of controversy. According to an authentic narration, the Prophet, while returning from *hajjatul wida* (his last pilgrimage to Mecca), halted for rest at *ghadir khomm,* a place situated midway between Mecca and Madina. Here while delivering a sermon to the faithful he proclaimed: "Of whosoever I am a *mawla* (friend and patron) Ali is also their *mawla* . . . ." The Shiites controvert this narration and claim that the Prophet did not utter *mawla* (patron) but *vali* (vicegerent). Hence their claim that the Prophet nominated Ali as his heir but his place was usurped by the first three *khulafa* – Abu Bakr, Umar and Uthman, and therefore their succession is void and illegitimate. The Sunnites refute this and assert that the Prophet did not nominate anybody as his successor but left the matter to the community. Hence the tension between the Shiite doctrine of *imamat* and the Sunnite doctrine of *khilafat*. Cf. T.W. Arnold, *Caliphate* (Oxford, Clarendon Press, 1924); S. Ameer Ali, *The Spirit of Islam* (London; Christophers, 1922); and Hamid Enayat, *Modern Islamic Political Thought:* the Response of the Shii and Sunni Muslims to the Twentieth Century (London: MacMillan, 1982).
3. According to an *Ithna Ashari* account, the period of the disappearance or occultation of the Last Imam is divided into a period of *ghaibat-i-sughra* (lesser absence) and *ghaibat-i-kubra* (greater absence). Lesser absence means the first 70 years of his disappearance when the Imam was still visible to and in communion with his *vakils* (agents). The first agent was appointed by the Imam himself and then each of the rest appointed his successor. The period of greater absence is said to have started in 9401 AD when the fourth *vakil*, Ali bin Muhammad al-Samarri, died without naming a successor. This period is believed to last until the expected return of the Hidden Imam.
4. As cited in Ibn Babwaih, *Ikmaluddin wa Itmamun Ne'mah* (Najaf, 1384 AH).
5. Ismail Safavi was a descendant of Sheikh Safiuddin (1252-1334 AD), a Shiite saint at Ardbil, who claimed his descent from Ali

Ibn Abi Talib. Ismail had come to power in Persia with the help of Qizilbashes, a Turkoman tribe converted to Shiism.

6. For a discussion of Usuli-Akhbari debate see Said Amir Arjomand, *The Shadow of God and the Hidden Imam* (Chicago: Chicago University Press, 1984).
7. Hamid Algar, *Religion and State in Iran.*
8. *Mnakat* (purifier) is an obligatory alm collected at the rate of 2.5 per cent of the value of assets held over a period of 12 months from those who are in possession of a prescribed quantum of gold or silver or other assets; *ushr* is ten per cent of the produce of one's land to be given in charity; and *sahm-i-Imam* (the dues of the Imam) is voluntary offering of monetary aid to maintain the seminaries and the *tullab* who are regarded as the successors of the Imam.
9. This subject has been treated extensively in Shahrough Akhavi, *Religion and Politics in Contemporary Iran* (Albany: State University of New York Press, 1980); Nikki, R. Kiddi, ed., *Religion and Politics in Iran* (New Haven: Yale University Press, 1983); and Roy P. Mottahedeh, *The Mantle of the Prophet.* Religion and Politics In Iran (New York: Pantheon Books, 1985).
10. Faridun Adamiyyat, *Ideologiyy-i-Mashruta-i-Iran* (Tehran, 1962).
11. Hasan Arfa, *Under Five Shahs* (London: Murray, 1968).
12. Ruhullah Musavi al-Khomeini, *Kalam-i-Imam,* Vol. 6,p. 33.
13. Their exemption from compulsory military service continues in the Islamic Republic provided they sign a bond undertaking to render teaching service under the Ministry of Education for at least five years after their graduation.

3

The Political Charter of Radical Shiism

Constitutionalism in the Islamic World

For centuries Islamic countries have been governed by the law of *shariat* which has been their moral, civil and criminal code. It is akin to the common law or customary law of Europe binding equally upon rulers and the ruled. Even the mightiest ruler could not dare alter or abrogate it or defy it openly. Civil and judicial authorities could interpret and expand its rules but could create no new rules or change the established ones.

The notion of *qanun* in the sense of administrative rules and regulations that could be made, amended and repealed by state authorities was imported from Europe. Thus in modern Turkey *shariat* law and civil law came to coexist side by side. Religious law was enforced through religious courts and administrative regulations through administrative or civil courts. Next, modern concepts of *qanun-i-asaasi* (constitutional or fundamental law) and *mashruteh* (charter) were borrowed from Europe to safeguard against arbitrary rule, establish rule of law and protect civil liberties. In the beginning of the twentieth century first Turkey and then Iran were the first Muslim countries to undergo constitutional revolutions under the impact of modern education and growth of political consciousness. Both achieved written constitutions and parliamentarism. But constitutional government could not take roots because native culture was not compatible with it.

The Liberal and Theocratic Constitutions

To unfurl the true character of the 1979 Constitution of the Islamic Republic it is useful and necessary to compare it with the liberal constitution of 1906-07. The earlier constitution was a product of a constitutional revolution that did not aim at abolition of monarchy but rather limiting its power by the will of people and parliament. It was a carbon copy of the Belgian constitution of the day and incorporated all the ideals of European constitutionalism. It is another matter that the constitutional revolution failed and the constitutional instrument became a façade and a democratic revolution was blocked. On the other hand, the Constitution of the Islamic Republic is a product of anti-monarchical revolution aiming at abolition of the monarchy and rejection of western political ideas and ideals. Its organizing principle is not sovereignty of people but hegemony of a patrimonial class in the medieval style. The two instruments can be compared in following respects:

1. *Constitutionalism:* Both constitutions aim at realizing the ideal of a constitutional government. But while the earlier constitution embodied the purpose of creating a limited responsible government, rule of law and independence of the judiciary the latter constitution has a very different meaning and content of constitutionalism. First, it does not aim at creating a government limited by the will of people and parliament but its objective is to establish rule of a jurisconsult at

the head of a guardian class self-appointed and responsible unto itself. The constitution, the laws, and the executive, legislative and judicial powers are all subservient to and auxiliaries of the supreme power of the guardian class. It aims not at creating a constitutional democracy but a constitutional theocracy. The constitutional theory of the radical mujtahids is akin to that of Soviet or Chinese communism.

2. *Shiism as State Religion*: Shiism was first declared as the state religion of Iran in 1501. That tradition was incorporated in the Constitutional Supplement of 1907 not with the purpose of establishing a sectarian government but just as a concession to the liberal mujtahids who had supported the constitutional movement. It no doubt enjoined the king (now a ceremonial head) to be a follower and propagator of the twelver religion. Another concession made to the mujtahids was that parliamentary legislation will not be repugnant to the law of the *shariat* and for that purpose a panel of five eminent mujtahids was empowered to examine the conformity of each law of parliament with religious principles.

The Constitution of 1979 on the other hand declares Iran to be an *Islamic* republic whose government is organized on the basis of the leadership of a *valiyy-i-faqih* (guardian jurisconsult) and continuous exercise of *ijtihad*. The meaning and content of the term *Islamic* can only be defined with reference to Article 5 (the leadership clause) and Article 12 (the twelver clause). While constitutions of many Muslim countries merely proclaim Islam as a ceremonial state religion without any sectarian stipulations the Iranian Constitution of 1979 categorically declares the twelver religion with its accompaniment of the Jafari brand of jurisprudence to be the state religion of the republic and the rule of the guardian class of twelver mujtahids as its system of government. The outcome is the creation of a sectarian state governed by the religious class of a particular sect.

3. *Popular Sovereignty:* The Constitutional Supplement of 1907 unequivocally declared popular sovereignty as the source of all governmental authority and made the king an instrument of the popular will as embodied in the constitution. Article 26 declared that all powers of government emanate from the people and can be exercised only in accordance with the constitution. The constitution of 1979, however, proclaims divine sovereignty as the source of all power and popular sovereignty (in the sense of governmental self-management) is derived from divine sovereignty. Divine will is represented on earth by the will of the Leader (the guardian jurisconsult) and his will limits and control the government.

4. *Separation of Powers:* The Lockean principle of the separation of powers and checks and balances was devised in the days when absolute kings ruled. It was conceived to prevent concentration of authority in one person or organ and to keep each organ of government confined to its own constitutional sphere. The principle was first embodied in the 1789 constitution of the USA and from there it was imported into the Constitutional Supplement of 1907 in Iran. It is another matter that this constitutional separation remained a farce so long as absolute monarchy prevailed. The constitution of 1979 too proclaims separation of legislative, executive and judicial powers but in practice there is no separation at all but complete union of powers with the guardian class, as headed by the Leader, unifying, integrating, harmonizing and coordinating all the powers. The three branches of government are not really autonomous

organs under a supreme constitution but merely auxiliary instruments of clerical hegemony.

The office of the Leader is the great unifying and coordinating factor as the personal representatives of the Leader are appointed in every important organ of the state as well as public organizations who act like the eyes and ears of the centre of power.

5. *Judicial Independence:* The constitution of 1906 proclaimed due process and judicial independence. Under its Article 71 the civil courts were for the first time separated from the religious courts and thus was laid the foundation of a secular independent judiciary. The jurisdiction of the religious courts was limited to personal and family matters and to such other cases which were referred to them for their opinion by civil courts. But under the Pahlavis judicial independence was subverted like many other constitutional principles. So the tradition of a subservient judiciary is deep-rooted in Iran. The constitution of 1979 proclaims the ideal of Islamic justice and lays utmost emphasis on the righteousness, piety and independence of the judges. In practice, the judiciary must be committed to the ideology and purposes of the regime. Judicial independence is a fiction because judiciary is placed under the personal command and control of a *rais-i-quwwa-i-qaza'iyya* (President of the Judicial Power) who is appointed for a fixed term of five years by the Leader in his own discretion and works under personal command, direction, supervision and control of the Leader. The head of the judiciary in turn is responsible for direction, superintendence and control of the networks of courts and their personal placed under him. The judiciary is now almost wholly manned by graduates of religious seminaries and clerical notions of judicial independence,

due process and impartial dispensation of justice are entirely different from the Western notions.

6. *Civil Liberties:* The constitution of 1907 guaranteed a number of personal, civil, political and religious rights to individuals. But this guarantee was soon subverted by the return of absolutism. Thus civil liberties in Iran have always been in jeopardy. The constitution of 1979 has included a lengthy bill of rights like many non-democratic constitutions. The enjoyment of these rights is subject to conformity with the ideology and purposes of the regime. Further, they exist by the leave of the regime. Their guarantee is neither absolute nor sacrosanct; they can be limited or denied under the law as well as in exercise of discretionary authority vested in executive and judicial authorities. Judicial remedies are seriously hampered by the operation of draconian laws such as the electoral laws, the law on Trade Unions, Associations and the Political Parties, and the Press Law.

7. *Constitutional Supremacy:*To provide for the sanctity and immutability of the constitution the instrument of 1906-07 prescribed a rigid amending procedure. A proposal for a constitutional amendment could be initiated by a two-third majority in the two chambers of the National Consultative Assembly acting separately or jointly. The proposal was then to be ratified by a Constituent Council elected upon a royal proclamation.

Since the constitution of 1979 is really a charter of clerical hegemony, therefore, its amending procedure is more rigid than ever conceived. The official religion of the state, the religious principles of government and the institution of *vilayat-i-faqih* have been excluded from the amending process. Under Article 177 amending power is primarily vested in the guardian class as presided over by the Leader and parliament and people have been assigned a secondary role. A proposal for a constitutional amendment can only be initiated by the Leader in consultation with the Board for the Identification of the Expediency of the System, the topmost policy-planning organ of the state. He will then direct the President of the Republic to submit the proposal for the consideration of a *Shura-i-Baznigariyy-i-Qanun-i-Asaasi* (Council for the Revision of the Fundamental Law).This grand council is composed of all the members of the Guardian Council, the heads of the three branches of government, the members of the Board for the Identification of the Expediency of the System, five members from the Assembly of Experts on Leadership, ten members to be nominated by the Leader, three members of the Presidential Cabinet, three members from the judicial branch, ten members of the Islamic Consultative Assembly and three professors chosen from among university professors. If approved by the Constitutional Revision Council the draft amendment or amendments must be resubmitted for perusal and signatures of the Leader. If approved and signed by the Leader the same must be submitted for a vote of the people in a national referendum held for that purpose. If ratified by an absolute majority of the people the amendment or amendments shall become a part of the constitution. It is clear that the substance of a proposed amendment must command the approval of the Leader before it is put to the vote of the people.

8.*Political Participation:* In feudal Iran universal adult franchise was unthinkable since in a class-ridden society the lower strata were not considered worthy of the right to vote. The first electoral law passed by the National Consultative Assembly in 1906 restricted the franchise to the following six strata of Iranian society:

1. Members of the royal family and the Qajar nobles
2. Mujtahids and *tullab* (students of religious seminaries)
3. Aristocrats and gentlemen
4. Traders and merchants
5. Landlords and cultivators; and
6. Members of professions and artisan guilds.

However, under the third electoral law enacted by the National Consultative Assembly in 1911 property and educational qualifications were abolished and universal male franchise introduced. Females were given the right to vote for the first time in 1962. But for most of the Pahlavi era parliamentary elections were unfree and unfair as they were manipulated by the agent of the central government to allow only the loyalists of the regime to be elected. That tradition has persisted in the Islamic regime too.

The constitution of 1979 has introduced universal adult franchise and created wider avenues of political participation but the entire system looks like the plebiscitary Dictatorship of the bygone era. The people vote frequently to choose their national parliament, the President of the Republic, the Assembly of Experts on Leadership, the local consultative councils and take part in national referendums. All Iranians of 17 years of age and above are eligible to vote and of a specified age able to stand as candidates. But eligibility criteria and the electoral procedures have so many loopholes that they can be used arbitrarily to favour the prodigal sons and to exclude the dissenters, opponents and non-favourites.

Like in the command systems of the bygone era membership in elective bodies is a reward for loyalty to the regime.

Source of Authority and Legitimacy

The Constitution of the Islamic Republic is a neotraditional charter of paternalistic government embodying the political ideas and ideals of radical Shiism. The core principle of this constitution is the principle of *vilayat-i-faqih* (the guardianship of jurisconsult). The *Valiyy-i-Amr* (the Custodian of Affairs) is formally designated as the Leader of the Islamic Revolution and the Custodian of the Affairs of the Muslims of the World. He governs by divine right and therefore governs absolutely. He is the sole source of authority and legitimacy in the system. His authority is at best scriptural and charismatic. He has a divine halo around him. His authority is therefore regarded as sacred and sacrosanct, unquestionable and irrevocable. The regime of the *vilayat-i-faqih* thus created is not only authoritarian but totalitarian in its scope. It claims to control all aspects of the individual and social life totally in accordance with the ideology of the regime.

Reference

1. For more details see Hamid Algar, *The Constitution of the Islamic Republic of Iran* (Albany: the State University of New York Press, 1980); and Amir Said Arjomand, "The Constitution of the Islamic Republic of Iran" in *The Encyclopaedia Iranica,* Vol. 6, ed. by Ehsan Yarshater (Costa Mesa, California: Mazda Publications, 1993).

4

The Guardianship of the Juriscounsult

The Place of the Leader

Article 2 of the Constitution of the Islamic Republic declares that "The Islamic Republic is a system of government founded on the principle of *imamat* and *rahbari* (leadership) based on the exercise of continuous *ijtihad* by the fully qualified *fuqaha* (religious jurists) in accordance with the Holy Book and the sayings of the infallible Imams."

This ideal of traditional religious government is operationalized by Article 5 of the Constitution which declares that during the disappearance of the Hidden Imam the governance of the state and leadership of the community in all spiritual and temporal matters is vested in a "Just and pious *faqih* (religious jurist) who is well aware of the conditions of his time, courageous, capable of governance and a statesman." In common parlance he is called *rahbar* (the leader) but he is formally designated as the *valiyy-i-amr-i-Muslimeen-i-Jahan wa Rahbar-i-Inquilab-i-Islami* (Custodian of the Affairs of the Muslims of the World and the Leader of the Islamic Revolution). Like the philosopher-king of

Plato's ideal state he is at the summit of the political system. He is the repository of absolute authority of the Imams. He personifies the unity of the church and state and he is the focus of the supreme loyalties of the faithful.

To understand the status and role of the Leader one must grasp Khomeini's theory of *vilayat-i-faqih* (guardianship of the jurisconsult). Khomeini's doctrine goes beyond the medieval doctrine of *vilayat-i-amma* (the duty of the mujtahids to perform religious and charitable functions on behalf of the Imams. Khomeini condemned clergy's isolation from politics and boldly declared that during the disappearance of the Hidden Imam the political leadership of the twelver community is neither suspended nor dispensed with; it is simply devolved upon his trustees the mujtahids. It is their duty to govern the community in accordance with the religious ordinances. Khomeini's reasoning in favour of a government by the mujtahids runs like this:

1. What is the best form of government for Muslims? Only the Islamic government is most suitable for the Muslims.

2. The essence of an Islamic government does not lie in its formal constitutional-legal structures but in the quality of its leadership, righteousness, piety and competence. This quality is available only in the mujtahids who alone can provide best government. Hence

3. It is the duty of the mujtahids to establish a just government. The government by a *faqih* is nothing but the performance of a divinely ordained duty.

The *vilayat* of the mujtahids is derived from the *imamat* of the Hidden Imam and the *imamat* of the Hidden Imam is derived from the *risalat* (mission) of the holy Prophet. The mujtahids are, therefore, the legatees and trustees of the divine authority of the Prophet and his holy descendants. The *valiyy-i-faqih* (the guardian jurisconsult) as the living counterpart of the Hidden Imam is to wield and exercise his authority in both spiritual and temporal matters. His authority is, therefore, divine, sacred and sacrosanct, unlimited and illimitable and inviolable and irrevocable. To preserve the sanctity of this office the Islamic Penal Code was amended in 1996 to provide that "Any contempt of the principle of *vilayat-i-faqih* is tantamount to a contempt of the Prophet and the Imams and is punishable by death."[1]

The Choice of the Leader

Article 107 of the Constitution of 1979 had laid down *marja'yyat* as the first and foremost condition for choice of a mujtahid as Leader. That alone can safeguard clerical hegemony. Only an acknowledged *marja'-i-taqlid* (source of emulation) possessing the qualities expected of a leader can be considered for a choice. That excludes non-mujtahids from competition for the supreme office. In case no such person was available, a *shura-i-rahbari* (leadership collegium) may be elected to perform the functions of the Leader. In 1979 no person could match Ayatullah Khomeni either as a *marja'-i-taqlid* or as a statesman. So he was coopted as Leader for life by the universal consensus of the community. After the Revolution of 1979 his followers began calling him as *Imam* because he was acknowledged as being the trustee and counterpart of the Hidden Imam. This term was lavishly used for eminent Sunnite scholars and jurists but it was considered sacriligeous to apply this term to a twelver. After the death of Khomeini in 1989 none of the theologian-jurists was found to be fit to step into the shoes of the departed Imam. So in 1989 Article 107 of the constitution was amended to drop the condition of *marja'iyyat* for the choice of the Leader and the provision regarding election of a leadership collegium in case of lack of consensus over the choice of the Leader was also scrapped for fear of outbreak of an inner power struggle among its members. The amended Article 107 reads:

> "After the exalted *marja-i-taqlid* and the great Leader of the World Islamic Revolution and the founder of the Islamic Republic of Iran the Greatest Symbol of God Imam Khomeini, who was acknowledged by an overwhelming majority of the people as their *marja'* and *rahbar,* the choice of the Leader is the responsibility of popularly elected *Khobregan* (experts). The *Khobregan-i-rahbari* (Experts on Leadership) shall discuss and consult among themselves over the names of all jurists who possess qualities described under Article 5 and 109. If they find anybody as most learned in religious ordinances and jurisprudence or social and political matters or commanding mass popularity or having extraordinary eminence in respect of qualities mentioned under Article 109 they will elect him and introduce him as the Leader. The Leader so elected by the Experts shall assume *vilayat-i-amr* (governance of the affairs of the community) and all responsibilities associated with his office"

The *majlis-i-khobregan-i-rahbari* (the Assembly of Experts on Leadership) was first elected in 1982 to select Ayatullah Khomeini's successor. Since then it has been elected for eight-year terms consecutively. The election and composition of the Assembly is prescribed by a law passed by the Islamic Consultative Assembly and it is empowered to determine its own rules of procedure. The strength of the Assembly is fixed at one member for each block of 50,000 voters in each of the 28 provinces of Iran. Thus the strength of the Assembly varies from

The Leadership Structure in the Islamic Republic

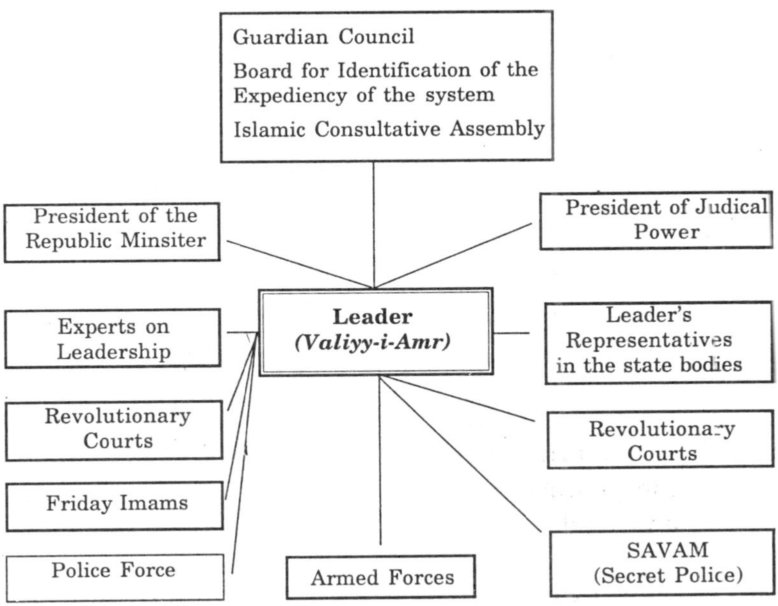

census to census. The present strength is fixed at 86. The Experts are elected by the people directly and under the law only qualified mujtahids can be allowed to become candidates. They are required to be well-informed and must be committed to the clerical regime.

The Assembly resembles the Accession Council in the UK (composed of all the members of Privy Council who on the death of a sovereign immediately meet in London to proclaim the accession of his successor). Its function during the life-time of an incumbent Leader is to hold an annual meeting at the spiritual capital of Qum, which is the seat of this body, to consider ways and means of strengthening the institution of Imamist leadership. Membership of this Assembly is a boon for such mujtahids who do not hold a post in the state. They are paid lavish salaries and allowances. The last election took place on 23 October 1998.

The qualifications and qualities of the Leader as laid down under Article 109 of the Constitution are:

1. Necessary academic competence to issue *fatwa* (legal opinions) in most branches of twelver jurisprudence.

2. Righteousness and piety necessary for the leadership of the twelver community, and

3. Proper political and social knowledge, statesmanship, courage, administrative competence and enough capability to command and lead.

Totalitarian Scope of Leader's Authority

The Leader has been vested with sweeping powers and the lower echelons of power are enjoined to work in subordination to and direction of the Leader. As listed under Article 110 the powers and functions which the Leader exercises in his own discretion are:

1. Determination of the macro policies of the Islamic Republic in consultation with the Board for the Identification of the Expediency of the System.

2. Supervision over proper implementation of public policies.

3. Issuing proclamations for holding popular referendums.

4. Supreme command of the armed forces of the republic.

5. Declaration of war and making of peace.

6. Appointment, dismissal and acceptance of the resignations of the religious jurists on the Guardian Council; the head of the Judiciary; the head of the Radio and Television of the Islamic Republic; the chief of the joint staff; the commander of the Revolutionary Guards; and the commanders of the armed forces and police force.

7. To settle differences among and to coordinate the functioning of the three branches of government.

8. To iron out the difficulties of the system which cannot be removed in the ordinary course of administration through the mediation of the Board for the Identification of the Expediency of the System.

9. To sign a proclamation for the appointment of the President of the Republic after he is duly elected by the people.

10. To sign a proclamation to the dismissal of the President of the Republic after the National Supreme Court has ruled for his dismissal on ground of dereliction of duty or on a vote of the Islamic Consultative Assembly confirming his incompetence to carry out the duties of this office in accordance with Article 89; and

11. Grant of pardon or remission of punishments of the convicts within the limits of the law on the recommendation of the President of the Judicial Power. The Leader is empowered to delegate some of his powers to officers subordinate to him.

In sum, the authority system of *vilayat-i-faqih* is dependent upon and made operative through five principal pillars and other auxiliary organizations: (1) the loyal Revolutionary Guards and the armed forces of the Republic; (2) the Assembly of Experts on Leadership; (3) the Islamic Consultative Assembly; (4) the Presidency of the Republic; and (5) the judiciary. The Leader is omnicompetent and omnipresent loyalist through his personal loyalties and through his personal representatives posted in all state and public organizations.

Reference

1. The concept of *vilayat-i-faqih* has been explained and elaborated by Khomeini's disciples, e.g. Husein Ali Muntazeri, *Vilayat-i-Faqih ya Hukumat-i-Islami,* 2 Volumes (Qum : Entesharaat-i- Islami, 1980) ; Murtaza Muttaheri, *Imamat-o-Rahbari* (Tehran: Sadra, 1994); and M. Javad Bahonar, *Mawaze'-i-Ma dar Vilayat-o-Rahbari* (Tehran: Farhang-i-Islami, 1994).

5

The Islamic Consultative Assembly

Parliamentary Elections and Composition

Legislative power in the Islamic Republic is exercised in two ways: By the Islamic Consultative Assembly by enacting laws and by the electorate by approving or disapproving measures put to them in a national referendum. The Islamic Consultative Assembly is composed of members elected by the people on the basis of universal adult franchise from territorial constituencies. The term is four years and the current strength is fixed at 290. The constitution has mandated that parliamentary elections be held ahead of the expiry of the term of an existing Assembly so that there is no interrugnum between two parliaments.

The Assembly is unicameral but three-tiered. At the top is the Guardian Council, the super chamber of parliament, which is the controller of parliamentary and presidential elections, vested with plenary power to approve nominations and supervise and control the electoral process from the beginning till the end. It is also the custodian of parliament in that no parliamentary bill can become law unless it is vetted and declared valid by it within ten days of it transmission by the Assembly. It is also the supreme constitutional court in that it is vested with, plenary power to declare an act of parliament as null and void on grounds of repugnancy to the *shariat* or the Fundamental Law.

The Islamic Consultative Assembly

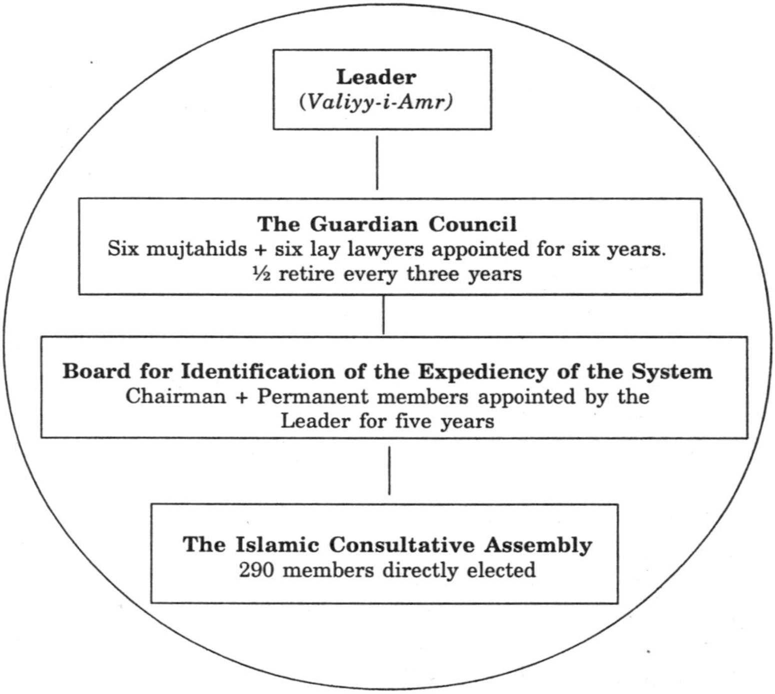

The second tier, interposed between the Guardian Council and the Islamic Consultative Assembly, is yet another appointed body designated as the Board for the Identification of the Expediency of the System. The Board was originally conceived as an arbitrator between the Guardian Council and the Islamic Consultative Council in cases where the former vetoes a bill but the latter does not agree to it. In due course it also became the highest consultative and policy-planning forum of the state as well as an independent ordinance-making authority.

Following the precedent set by the electoral law of 1909, the Constitution of 1979 has reserved some seats in the Assembly for the non-Muslim religious minorities in Iran. One seat is reserved for Zorostrians, one for the Jews, one for the Assyrians and Chaldeans taken together, and one for the Armenians of southern Iran and one for the Armenians of northern Iran. They are exempted from eligibility criteria applied to Muslim candidates.

Parliamentary elections are held in two rounds in the French style. In the first round only such candidates are declared elected who secure an absolute majority of votes and at least one-third of the total votes cast in their constituencies. Polling for the unfilled seats is held in a second round. Candidates twice the number of unfilled seats who secured the highest number of votes in the first round are fielded as candidates in the second round. To win in the second round not absolute but a relative majority or plurality of votes is required. Filing of nomination papers from more than one constituency is by rule an electoral offence and the election result of a candidate found guilty of committing this offence is cancelled. Every Iranian citizen of seventeen years or more who is not insane is eligible to exercise his franchise in election. To become a candidate in parliamentary elections, a person must be an Iranian citizen, a believing and practising Muslim, physically and mentally sound, and be of a minimum of thirty years of age but of not more than 75 years. The holders of offices of profit are barred from contesting elections.

Besides, certain categories of persons who have been barred from contesting elections under the law are: (1) supporters and loyalists of the former royal regime; (2) land grabbers who got the properties of deceased persons registered in their names; (3) members and supporters of the political parties and groups declared unlawful by the Islamic Republic; (4) persons found guilty of acting against the interests of the Islamic Republic; (5) persons convicted by a court of law for committing the offence of renouncing the Islamic faith; (6) persons of proven corruption and misconduct; (7) persons convicted by the courts of law for committing offences under the law of *shariat*; (8) drug addicts; (9) destitutes; and (10) ministers, high officials, members of the Senate and the National Consultative Assembly of the Pahlavi era; and the office-bearers and functionaries of the official political parties floated by the Pahlavi regime.

The process of a parliamentary election starts with the appointment of a five-member Central Electoral Supervisory Body by the Guardian Council. This Body works in coordination with the Interior Ministry which is responsible for the conduct of elections. Out of the five members one must compulsorily be a member of the Guardian Council who presides over the proceedings of the Central Supervisory Body and has a controlling voice. The Central Body is responsible for direction, supervision and control of the entire electoral process right from the stage of the clearance of nominations by the Guardian Council up to the end of polling. The Central Electoral Supervisory Body nominates Provincial Electroal Bodies one each for each of the twenty-eight provinces of Iran. The Provincial Electoral Supervisory Body in turn appoints a three-member Constituency Electoral Supervisory Body one each for each of the parliamentary constituencies in the concerned province. The Constituency Electoral Supervisory Bodies are responsible for overseeing the conduct of polling, counting of votes and declaration of results. The decisions of these bodies in all matters are deemded as final and binding except in such cases where polling has been suspended or cancelled in a whole constituency or a booth or a number of booths or where the nomination papers of a candidate have been rejected. All such cases are referred to the Central Electoral Supervisory Body for review and disposal. If a candidate raises an objection against the rejection of his nomination papers before the list of candidates is finalized the complaint is referred to the Guardian Council for review and disposal. Its decision is regarded as final, binding and non-appealable.[1]

From the above it becomes apparent that the electoral procedure and administration of the clerical regime is not much different from that of the former Fascist or Communist regimes. Fool-proof mechanisms of controlled elections ensure that only the faithful and loyal are allowed to become members of elective bodies.

The Speaker of the Islamic Consultative Assembly

As soon as the results of parliamentary elections are declared the members-elect assemble in Tehran and elect a temporary presidium of the Islamic Consultative Assembly composed of two oldest members as president and vice-president and two younger members as secretaries. This presidium is akin to the speaker *pro tempore* in democratic countries. The presidium administers the prescribed oath to the elected members. After this oath-taking the parliamentarians leave *en mass* to the tomb of Imam Khomeini in the Behesht-i-Zohra cemetery in the south of Tehran to pay their homage to the founder of the Islamic Republic. Coming back to the premises of the Assembly in the north of Tehran a permanent presidium (with a president or speaker, two vice-presidents or deputy speakers, six secretaries and three *rapporteurs*) is elected by a two-thirds majority of the members-elect and all the members of the Guardian Council present and voting. Election is by an absolute majority of votes. The President of the Assembly (or the speaker) is accorded the customary status, powers and privileges available to the presiding officers of democratic chambers.

Parliamentary Standing Commissions

The election of the Presidium is followed by the appointment of Parliamentary standing commissions whose number, designations, composition and jurisdiction are defined in the Code of Internal Procedure of the Islamic Consultative Assembly. Each of these Commissions is concerned with one particular field dealt with by one ministry or public organization. The presidium of the Assembly first collects the resumes' of members interested in serving on particular commissions and circulates them among the general body for perusal and comments. Then the members group themselves according to their choice of subjects to consider the resumes. If the number of candidates aspiring to serve on a particular commission exceeds the authorized strength then heads of ad hoc groups and members of the presidium of the house together decide the composition of the commissions by a vote of majority. Under the rules each member of the Assembly is required to serve at least on one standing commission. Membership of an additional commission is permissible but without a vote.

In 2004 there were some 26 standing commissions relating to education and training; Islamic guidance, arts and mass media; administrative management and public services; economics, finance and cooperation; planning and budget; oil; industries and mines; employment and social affairs; healthcare, social security and Red Crescent; post, telegraph and power; commerce and public distribution, agriculture and rural development; the Commission of Article 90; the Commission of Article 70; the Court of Audit, Finance and Financial Affairs; the charitable public foundations established after the Revolution; public inquiries; parliamentary procedure; laws enacted during the pre-revolutionary era and laws enacted by the Revolutionary Council; culture and higher education; and human rights.

As soon as the standing commissions are constituted each commission meets to elect from among itself one chairman, two vice-chairmen, two secretaries and one *rapporteur*.

Each commission has a minimum of nine and a maximum of fifteen members. But the human rights commission has 17. The commission of Article 90 has a minimum of 15 and maximum of 31 members. The commissions on audit, work and social affairs have a maximum of seven members each.

The Commission of Article 90 is meant to perform functions mentioned under Article 90 of the Constitution. It reads "If any person has a grievance concerning the functioning of the Islamic Consultative Assembly or the executive branch or the judicial branch he may submit his complaint in writing to the Commission of Article 90. If the complaint concerns the Islamic Consultative Assembly the Assembly is duty-bound to consider it and give a satisfactory reply. If it concerns the executive or the judicial branch it will be forwarded to the concerned branch for consideration and reply within a reasonable time limit. Replied received by the Assembly will then be communicated to the parties concerned. If the complaint involves the general public the result of the inquiry will be published in the official media for general information. If a complaint concerns the Commission's own jurisdiction it will investigate it and report the result to its own presidium who will then transmit it to the speaker of the Assembly who will then direct that the matter be placed on the agenda of the next meeting of the Assembly for consideration and decision.

Conduct of Parliamentary Business

Like democratic chambers the Iranian Assembly too spends most of its time on deliberation over matters of public importance, debate over bills and motions, raising parliamentary questions and putting interpellations to individual ministers or cabinet as a whole or the President of the Republic. For transaction of parliamentary business and adoption of measures a two-thirds majority of members and the presence of the members of the Guardian Council is compulsory. The quorum to keep debates going is fixed at one-half of the membership.

Before the start of parliamentary business of the day members are given half an hour to raise questions of their choice. If it is an interpellation against a single minister and taken up for debate two hours are allotted; if it is directed against a group of ministers or the whole cabinet four hours are provided.

Each bill introduced in the Assembly gets a first hearing in the subject-related standing commission. After the commission has reported the measure is taken up in the whole house for a second reading. After a third reading the bill is either returned to the standing commission for reconsideration within five days or it is voted upon finally. When a bill is passed by the house it must be submitted to the Guardian Council for vetting and approval. The Guardian Council can either approve it or reject it stating its reasons within ten days. Ten more days may be taken, if considered necessary. If the bill is not approved by the Council it will be returned to the house with its objections for reconsideration. If the house removes the objectionable points the bill will become law after the signatures of the President of the Republic.

Parliamentary Functions and Role

The Assembly is competent to make laws within its jurisdiction and debate and approve the executive budget. The Assembly cannot pass a law that is contrary to the religion of the state or violative of the Fundamental Law. The Assembly is also competent to explain and interpret its own laws without prejudice to the right of the judiciary to do so in the course of delivering judgments. It is also a forum for discussion of all matters of public importance. All treaties, agreements, accords and contracts must be ratified by the Assembly before their implementation. Similarly contracting of loans abroad or making of grants to domestic or foreign entities must also command the consent of the Assembly. After each parliamentary election and after each reconstitution of the ministry, the President of the Republic presents each member of cabinet to the Assembly and seeks a vote of confidence and later seeks a vote of confidence for the whole cabinet. Parliamentary confirmation is necessary before the ministers take charge of their ministries/departments. The Assembly controls the executive by means of parliamentary questions and debates, raising interpellations (*isteezah*), and censure and no-confidence motions against individual ministers or the whole cabinet or the President of the Republic.

One of the most important functions of the Assembly is to act as a forum for articulating the grievances and complaints of the public and getting them redressed by the government. Under Article 90 of the Fundamental Law any citizen who is aggrieved by the functioning of either the Assembly or the executive branch or the judiciary may submit his complaint in writing to the speaker of the Assembly. The Assembly has a standing commission named the Commission of Article 90 to consider such matters and report to the whole house which then takes a decision which is transmitted to the complainant. If the complaint concerns the other branches it will be referred to them for investigation and report. The report will then be communicated to the parties concerned. If it concerns the general public it will be published in the official media for general information.

Guardian Council

The Guardian Council is superimposed upon the popularly elected house which is vested with the power of constitutional review of parliamentary legislation besides controlling the elections to the Islamic Consultative Assembly, the Presidency of the Republic, the Assembly of Experts on Leadership and national referendums.

The Guardian Council is composed of (1) six mujtahids (religious jurists) appointed by the Leader; (2) six lay lawyers nominated by the President of the Judicial Power and confirmed by the Islamic Consultative Assembly. The members are appointed for a term of six years but half of the members of each category retire every three years and they are eligible for reappointment. Although an appointed body the Guardian Council is an integral part of parliament and its overlord and watchdog. The Islamic Consultative Assembly can neither meet nor transact any business unless all the members of the Guardian Council are present, except in two matters (1) verification of the credentials of the newly elected members, and (2) voting for confirmation of six lay lawyers as members of the Guardian Council.

Every bill passed by the Islamic Consultative Assembly is required to be submitted to the Guardian Council who will either approve it so it is sent for the signatures of the President of the Republic and becomes an act; or if the Council has reservations about the bill it will communicate its objections to the Assembly within ten days of receipt of a bill and ask the Assembly to reconsider it. If the assembly meets the objections of the Council it is approved by the Council, signed by the President of the Republic and becomes law. If, however, the Assembly does not agree with the objections of the Council a deadlock ensues between the two bodies. In this case the controversial bill is referred by the Leader to the Board for Identification of the Expediency of the System for arbitrating between the two and resolving the dispute. A bill can be vetoed on grounds of repugnancy to the law of *shariat* only by a majority vote of the religious jurists on the Guardian Council. Similarly, a bill can be rejected on grounds of constitutional invalidity by a majority vote of the six lay lawyers on the Council. Besides, the Council interprets the constitution without prejudice to the right of higher judiciary to do so and conflicts of ruling are resolved through arbitration by the expediency Board.

The Board for the Identification of the Expediency of the System

This is the third tier of the Islamic Consultative Assembly. It is a curious institution the like of which is not found either in the Christian West or the Islamic East. It is an offshoot of political *ijtihad*. It may be described as the *taqayya* board and subscribes to the Hobbesian and Machiavellian concept of separation of religion and politics. The underlying idea, endorsed by Imam Khomeini himself, is that when ethical and religious orthodoxy conflicts with the interest of the nation and state it is the supreme duty of the political authorities to accord primacy to the national interest. The body was first appointed by Imam Khomeini in 1988 as an arbitration forum for ironing out intra-regime differences and adjudicating conflicting claims of competing authorities. The experiment proved useful and worthy. So after the death of Imam Khomeini it was accorded a statutory status through a constitutional amendment in 1989 and was interposed between the Guardian Council and the Islamic Consultative Assembly. In accordance with Article 112 of the Constitution the Board is responsible for identifying the expediency of the system in cases where the Guardian Council rejects a parliamentary bill on grounds of repugnancy to the Islamic *shariat* or violation of the Constitution and the Assembly does not agree with the Council's veto. The Board strives (through the exercise of continuous *ijtihad*) to strike a balance between dogma and reality by according primacy to the concrete interests of the system over abstract moral principles.

The Board consisting of a chairman and permanent, ad hoc and invitee members is appointed by the Leader by a proclamation. The Board has since 1998 been presided over by the veteran Akbar Hashemi Rafsanjani. The Board is composed of top-ranking office-holders of the regime; the heads of the three branches of government, the mujtahids of the Guardian Council; some other public figures and the minister in charge of the ministry or head of a public organization whose affairs are on the agenda of the Board for time-being as well as the head of the concerned parliamentary standing commission as ad hoc members. The functions of the Board may be summarized as (1) arbitrating between the Guardian Council and the Islamic Consultative Assembly over controversial bills; (2) advising the Leader on matters referred by him for its opinion; and (3) undertaking macro policy-planning in important sectors of national life.[2] Finally, the Board is also conceived as a standby legislative authority It can promulgate instant rules, regulations and laws in its own right. Some instances are: rules framed in 1989 to prevent the wastage of the subsidized wheat, wheat-flour and *naan*; the law to curb trafficking in drugs and narcotics; or the 1990 law creating an Administrative Court for the Judiciary.

Popular Referendums

Popular referendums are provided to ascertain the wishes of the people on issues referred to them by the regime. The conduct of referendums is regulated by a Law on Referendums enacted by the Islamic Consultative Assembly in 1989. A proposal for holding a referendum may be initiated either by the President of the Republic or by one hundred members of the Islamic Consultative Assembly and must be ratified by at least two-third majority of all members of parliament. A referendum so proposed is conducted by the Interior Ministry in consultation with the Guardian Council and polling is limited to one day spread over ten hours. The Interior Ministry is responsible for administrative arrangements and the Guardian Council for supervision over polling. All Iranian citizens of 17 years and above are eligible to vote in "yes" or "no". The verdict of the people has first to be ratified by the Leader then transmitted for implementation to the President of the Republic.

Local Consultative Councils

Articles 100-106 of the Constitution have provided for the creation of a network of local consultative councils at the village, block of villages, town, city, country and province levels to provide for local participation in local government, development and management of local utilities. In addition, there is a Central Consultative Council for the Provinces composed of one representative from each of 28 provinces to formulate inter-provincial development projects and to submit the same to the Islamic Consultative Assembly for approval.

In accordance with the constitutional provisions, a Law on the Local Consultative Councils was passed by the Islamic Consultative Assembly in 1982 but internal strife did not permit its implementation. Local elections were held for the first time on 1 February 1999. The turnout was about 60 per cent for some 200,000 local council seats. The reformist faction of the regime who were at the height of their popularity at the time bagged most of the seats. In the second elections held on 28 February 2003 the turnout was merely 39 per cent indicating voter apathy and this time the conservatives garnered most of the seats.

References

1. The Law on the Supervision of the Guardian Council over Elections to the Islamic Consultative Assembly was passed in 1986. The Code of Internal Procedure of the Majlis was last revised in 1986. The Law on the Supervision of the Guardian Council over the Election of the President of the Republic was passed in 1981.
2. *Kaihaan-i-Havai*, 24 December 1997.

6

The President of the Republic

The President of the Republic has been accorded the topmost position in the system next to the Leader under Article 113 of the Constitution. As the chief executive it is his duty to execute the constitution of the republic and enforce its laws faithfully and to preside over the administration of the state except in matters reserved by the constitution for the Leader. But the independence and authority of the executive president is quite limited because he has to work with two bosses: the Leader and the Islamic Consultative Assembly working under the tutelage of the Guardian Council. Although the principle of separation of legislative and executive powers has been borrowed from the earlier constitution in practice it is just superficial. Both the powers are unified, coordinated and controlled by the Leader assisted by the Guardian Council and the judiciary. In the same way the principle of ministerial responsibility too has been retained from the earlier constitution and the Assembly is empowered to dismiss a minister or the entire cabinet by a vote of no-confidence and impeach the President of the Republic.

The President of the Republic performs his functions with the aid of his cabinet composed of ministers which remains in office during the pleasure of the President and the confidence of the Assembly. In addition, the President can appoint a number of vice-presidents who are accountable to him. The first vice-president looks after cabinet affairs, presides over the meetings of the National Security Council and coordinates between the offices of several vice-presidents.

The Mode of Presidential Election

The President of the Republic is elected by the people directly for a term of four years. A candidate must be a natural-born Iranian citizen, must belong to the *Ithna Ashari* (twelver) religion, profess loyalty to the Islamic Republic and its constitution. The election is governed by a Law on Presidential Election passed by the Islamic Consultative Assembly in 1980. The Guardian Council has the prerogative of clearing candidates and supervising the poll.

To win a candidate must secure an absolute majority of votes dast in the first round of polling. In case no candidate obtains an absolute majority a second round is arranged the next Friday with two candidates who secured the most numerous votes in the first round. In case the top two withdrew from the contest then the next top will be fielded and the result will be decided by a relative majority or plurality of votes. By rule, a president must conclude one month before the expiry of the term of an incumbent president.

The Executive System of the Islamic Republic

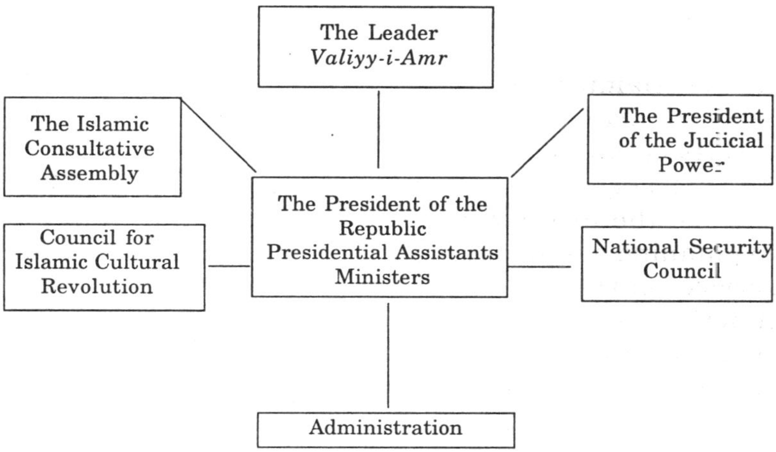

The President of the Republic can be dismissed by the Leader either on a vote of impeachment by the Islamic Consultative Assembly or on ground of incompetence or by the Leader in his own discretion on charges of dereliction of duty. The President may submit his resignation at will and will continue in office till his resignation is accepted. In case of death, dismissal, resignation or absence for more than two months, the first Assistant to the President, with the approval of the Leader, shall act as president. In case of his unwillingness to perform this duty any body else may be appointed as acting president. A successor must be elected within 50 days of occurrence of a vacancy.

The Role of the Executive President

The statutory powers and functions of the President of the Republic may be enumerated as: (1) to oversee the proper implementation of the constitution and the laws of the republic; (2) to direct, supervise and control the whole range of the activities of the administrative branch; (3) to sign or deputise somebody else to sign the treaties, agreements, protocols and contracts between Iran and other countries and international conventions and to implement them after retification by the Islamic Consultative Assembly; (4) to sign bills after clearance by the Guardian Council and the results of national referendums and to transmit them to concerned authorities for implementation; (5) to assume the direct responsibility for matters relating to planning and budgeting, the administration and the services of the state (and he may delegate some of his functions to others); (6) to accredit the diplomatic representatives of Iran to other countries and to receive the credentials of the diplomats from other countries; (7) to award state honours, prizes and medals; and (8) any other function assigned to him under the law.

The Presidential Cabinet

Soon after his election the President of the Republic selects his ministers and presents them individually and collectively to the Islamic consultative Assembly for a vote of confidence. Together they form the presidential cabinet. The President of the Republic alongwith his cabinet is collectively responsible before the Assembly. The President is required to seek a vote of confidence after each reshuffling or reconstitution of the cabinet and also before embarking on an important policy initiative.

Although the President of the Republic, the presidentialassistantsand ministers are constitutionally barred from seeking membership of the house they are allowed to participate in the deliberations of the house without a vote. The Assembly on its own may direct particular ministers or the entire team to be present in a particular meeting and listen to the views expressed by parliamentarians.

Any ten members of the Assembly are entitled to table an *interpellation* (a parliamentary motion seeking an explanation from the government; failure to give a satisfactory explanation leads to withdrawal of confidence; this motion was prevalent during the Third and Fourth French Republics). Failure to address the interpellation would likely lead to a motion of impeachment and dismissal from office. Impeached minister, or ministers, or the cabinet ceases to hold office. The impeached minister/ministers may not, as a rule, be included in the next reshuffled cabinet. An interpellation may also be directed against the President of the Republic by one-third members of the Assembly. If the President does not appear before the Assembly within a month and explain himself satisfactorily the Assembly may impeach him and he will be dismissed by the Leader upon such impeachment.

National Security Council

Article 176 of the Constitution (as amended in 1989) provided for the creation of a National Security Council under the chairmanship of the President of the Republic to take care of national security and territorial integrity of Iran. This body replaced the earlier body entitled the National Defence Council created under original Article 176 under the chairmanship of the Leader. Whereas the former Council's jurisdiction was limited to external security and it had no doubt played a crucial role in strategic planning and coordination during the long-drawn Iraq-Iran War, the newer body's jurisdiction covers both external and internal security. The National Security Council is presided over by the President of the Republic or on his behalf by the First Assistant to the President. The Council is composed of the heads of the three branches of government, the chief of the staff of the armed forces, the head of the Planning and Budget Organization, two members nominated by the Leader, and ministers of foreign affairs, interior and information. The ministries and organizations represented on the Council are authorized to form departmental security councils dealing withtheir particular functional areas and to supplement and complement the work of the National Security Council.

Presidents of the Republic since 1980

1. Abol Hasan Bani Sadr; elected in January 1980
2. Muhammad Ali Rejai; elected in July 1981
3. Sayyid Ali Khamenei; elected in October 1982; re-elected in August 1985.
4. Akbar Hashemi Rafsanjani; elected in July 1989; re-elected in June 1993.
5. Sayyid Muhammad Khatami, elected in May 1997; re-elected in June 2001.
6. Mahmoud Ahmadi Nezhad; elected in August 2005.

The Armed Forces

In addition to organs of the state, the ideological apparatuses like the Ministry of Culture and Islamic Guidance, the Radio and Television, the Council for Cultural Revolution, etc. the regime is propped and upheld in the main by the loyal and committed Revolutionary Guards, the regular armed forces and the police force (1991 the three separate police forces namely the local *komitehs* or city police, the *shahrbani* and the gendarmerie were merged to form a single police force). The police force has sweeping power in fields of maintaining internal law and order, controlling traffic in narcotics and drugs and acting as the executive wing of the judiciary in enforcing the moral code of the regime in the society. The Revolutionary Guards were raised in 1979 on the orders of Ayatullah Khomeini as a counter-force in addition to the regular armed forces. The *Basij* (volunteers force) was also raised soof afterwards to assist the Revolutionary Guards in combating counter-revolutionary activities and to suppress the minority nationalities inhabiting the border regions of Iran. The *Basij* were merged with the Revolutionary Guards in 1980. The Revolutionary Guards in close tandem with the regular armed forces and the *Sazmaan-i-Ittelaat-o-Amniyyat-i-Meehan* – SAVAM [The Organization of Intelligence and Homeland Security] which is a direct successor of the notorious *Sazman-i-Amniyyat-o-Ittelaat-i-Kishwar*– SAVAK) [Origanization of State Intelligence and Security] of the Pahlavi regime. The appointment and dismissal of all personnel of the armed forces is vested in the Leader. They are ideologically committed to defend and uphold the clerical regime and are regularly indoctrinated by the Religious Corps of the Defence Ministry.

7

The Judicial Power

Islamization of the Judiciary

In pre-modern Iran there existed neither a unified body of law nor an integrated system of administration of justice. Justice was dispensed in accordance with the law of *shariat* by local *qazis* and mujtahids scattered throughout Iran. They decided the cases by applying the principles of the Jafari school of jurisprudence as well as local customs. Administration of justice was chaotic because of fragmented nature of judicial precedents, conflicting interpretations of the law and diversity of rulings. During the reign of Nasiruddin Shah Qajar the idea of enacting an Islamic personal law on the pattern of Muslim personal law in British India was mooted with a view to unifying the law but was never acted upon. However, after the Constitutional Revolution of 1906 two major departures were made from the traditional practice: for the first time a popularly elected parliament became empowered to make law in worldly affairs and for the first time civil courts were separated from religious courts and then the jurisdiction of the religious courts was restricted to adjudicating personal and family matters and giving advisory opinion on such cases as were referred to them by the civil courts. These advisory opinions were non-binding. Then in 1928 Reza Khan promulgated a French-style uniform civil code on an experimental basis, confirmed it in 1936 and abolished the religious courts altogether. Since 1979, however, the Islamic regime overturned the process of secularization by enjoining the complete Islamization of the legal and judicial system. Now courts of law are mostly headed by qualified mujtahids who apply the Islamic civil and penal codes as enacted by the Islamic Consultative Assembly during the early years of the Republic and modified from time to time.

Further, no law passed by the Assembly can be contrary to the *shariat* and their conformity is enforced through the medium of the Guardian Council. By sweeping judicial reforms the diverse courts of law were integrated into a unified judicial hierarchy headed at the top by a mujtahid designated as the President of the Judicial Power. Furthermore, strenuous efforts were made to remove duplication of jurisdiction between and among courts and to remove conflicts of rulings and judgments.

The process of Islamization was set in full motion in 1982 by an eight-point Proclamation issued by Imam Khomeini to all the authorities of the state. The eight points were:

1. Formulation, legislation and promulgation of the Islamic civil and penal codes with due care and utmost speed.

2. Speedy and effective scrutiny of the ability and competence of the judges, prosecutors and courts with a view to ensuring proper administration of justice and protecting the rights of the people.

3. Judges who fulfill the Islamic criteria must enforce the Islamic law throughout the country independently and without regard to anybody's status and all agents of the must abide by their judgments and execute their decrees.

4. Nobody is allowed to interrogate or detain any person even for a short period without an order issued by a judge in accordance with the *shariat*. Any such transgression of unauthorized detention shall be deemed to be an offence punishable under the law.

5. Nobody is entitled to encroach upon the movable or immovable property of any person without an order issued by a competent religious authority.

6. Nobody is allowed to enter the dwelling place or a shop or a factory without the permission of its owner and all forms of blackmailing shall be punishable under the law.

7. The above prohibition may be relaxed in relation to intrigues and conspiracies hatched against the Islamic Republic but even in such cases deviation from religious norms is impermissible; and;

8. The head of the *Diwan-i-A'liyy-i-Kishwar* (National Supreme Court) Agha Musavi Ardbili and the Prime Minister are duty-bound to receive the complaints of the people in regard to the above mentioned matters and refer the same to concerned authorities for investigation and redressal.[1]

The President of the Judicial Power

Under Article 157 of the Constitution (as amended in 1989) the Leader appoints a just and well-informed mujtahid possessing administrative abilities as the President of the Judicial Power for a term of five years to direct, supervise and control the functioning of the judicial branch.[2]

Judicial Hierarchy in the Islamic Republic

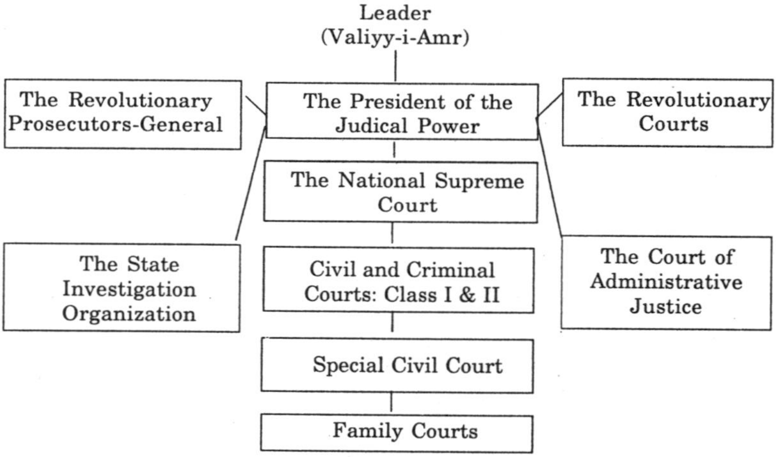

The statutory functions of the President of the Judicial Power are enumerated under Article 158 of the Constitution as:

1. To create the necessary infrastructure of the judicial systemcommensurat with responsibilities entrusted to it under Article 156 of the Constitution.

2. To prepare schemes of judicial reforms in consonance with the character of the Islamic Republic; and

3. To recruit pious and righteous mujtahids for appointment as judges and to make rules concerning their appointment, dismissal, remuneration, postings and transfers and the like in accordance with the law.

The National Supreme Court

The National Supreme Court is the highest court of the law with its seat in Tehran. Its main function is to see to it that the lower courts apply the law properly and justly and that they dispense justice impartially. It is also bound to perform such other functions assigned to it under the law and in accordance with rules framed by the President of the Judicial Power. The Supreme Court is headed by a chief justice who is appointed for a term of five years by the President of the Judicial Power in conslultation with the other judges of the Court.

In accordance with Article 173 of the Constitution (as amended in 1989) a Court of Administrative Justice has been created under the supervision of the President of the Judicial Power with its seat in Tehran to investigate complaints of the public against public employees, officers and agencies and against unjust and unfair rules, regulations and procedures and to settle the rights and claims of the citizens against the authorities.

The Revolutionary Courts

Revolutionary Courts were formed and Revolutionary prosecutors were appointed soon after the Revolution in 1979 to apprehend, prosecute and try the agents of the Pahlavi regime who were accused of committing atrocities against the people. These were regularized by the Law on the jurisdiction of the Revolutionary

Prosecutors and Revolutionary Courts passed by the Islamic Consultative Assembly in 1993. They are a permanent feature of the contemporary Iranian judicial system, operate under the supervision of the President of the Judicial Power, and dispense revolutionary justice in a draconian fashion.

The jurisdiction of the Revolutionary Prosecutors and Revolutionary Courts covers the following:

1. All offences committed against internal and external security of Iran, waging war against the Islamic Republic and Iran, waging war against the Islamic Republic and indulging in spreading corruption on earth (*fasad fil arz*).

2. Attempts to assassinate the leaders of the Islamic Republic.

3. All offences connected with trafficking the smuggling of drugs and narcotics.

4. All cases of killing or detaining or torturing the people to strengthen the Pahlavi regime and of suppression of the popular struggle against Pahlavi dictatorship.

5. All cases of plundering the public exchequer; and

6. All cases of profiteering and hoarding of essential commodities.

The Ministry of Justice

The Ministry of Justice is the nodal agency for dealing with grievance of the public against judicial mal-administration. Besides, it is also responsible for establishing lower-rung courts, defining their jurisdiction and arranging for their premises and personnel, in accordance with the law. Moreover, under Article 160 of the Constitution the Minister of Justice is responsible for ensuring coordination between the judicial and the legislative and executive branches.

Unlike other ministers the Minister of Justice is not the personal choice of the President of the Republic. He is obliged to select his justice minister only from a panel of names forwarded to him by the President of the Judicial Power. That means that the entire judicial establishment alongwith the ministry of justice has been placed under the indirect control and surveillance of the Leader.

The President of the Judicial Power is empowered to delegate his recruiting, administrative and financial powers in respect of non-judicial personnel to the Justice Minister who will perform them in his administrative capacity.

The State Investigation Organization

Sazmaan-i-baazrasiyy-i-kull-i-kishwar or the the State Investigation Organization is a carbon copy of the American Federal Bureau of Investigation (FBI). It was first created by the Shah as an adjunct of the State Security and Intelligence Agency (the dreaded SAVAK) in 1958 to investigate charges of corruption, administrative misconduct, dereliction of duty and disloyalty against royal ministers and high offieers. The organization survived the Revolution, was reorganized by the clerical regime and made an adjunct of the judicial branch. Under the relevant law passed by the Islamic Consultative Assembly in 1981 it is responsible for investigating charges of corruption and abuse and misuse of power by the administrative personnel of state ministries and public organizations, government-owned companies and revolutionary foundations. Besides, the organization undertakes routine checks on the administrative agencies periodically. Moreover, it is empowered to conduct an extraordinary inquiry into any case referred to it either by the Leader or the President of the Republic or the President of the Judicial Power or the Parliamentary Standing Commission of Article 90 or any minister or the head of the State Investigation Organization. Field units of this agency are located in almost all important government complexes, headquarters of public organizations and university campuses throughout the country.

References

1. Ruhullah Musavi al-Khomeini, *Saheefa-i-Nur*, vol. 17 (1985), pp.105-107.
2. The original constitution of 1979 had provided for a *Shura-i-Aliyy-i-Qazayi* (The Supreme Judicial Council) on the model of a similar institution provided under the 1958 constitution of the Fifth Republic of France. The body was meant to head and supervise the judicial system. However, a constitutional amendment passed in 1989 abolished it for being cumbersome and replaced it by a single head named *Rais-i-Quwwa-i-Qaza'iyya* (the President of the Judicial Power). The Law on the Powers and Functions of the President of the Judicial Power was passed by the Majlis in 1992.

8

The Political Parties in Iran

Responsible parliamentary government is inconceivable without the existence of a strong and stable parliamentary party system. A viable parliamentary party system is supported and sustained by party organizations having roots among the masses. The bane of Iranian politics ever since the Constitutional Revolution of 1906 has been the absence of a viable parliamentary party system as well as of broad-based party organizations operating on the basis of policy and principles. Most parties have been no more than coalescence of loyalists around personalities and cliques. Some reasons for this state were (1) the abject poverty, illiteracy and political exclusion of the masses; (2) the acute fragmentation of the Iranian society on class, ethnic, tribal, religious, sectarian and regional bases; (3) the self-regarding orientation and opportunism of the Iranians that prevents them from coming together for collective action for the attainment of collective goals; (4) the machinations and intrigues of both domestic and foreign vested interests which were bent upon subverting the constitutional experiment; and (5) the top of all was the suffocating role of despotic monarchy which suppressed civil liberties, banned political participation and eliminated all dissent and opposition.

The Origins of Iranian Parties

Political associations were formed for the first time in Iran during the constitutional period of 1905-1911.[1]

At the turn of the nineteenth century three distinct strata of the Iranian society the liberal intellectuals, the mujtahids and the *baazaris* (merchants) made a common cause against the atrocities of the reigning Qajar king. They formed a network of *anjumans* (associations) throughout the country to mobilize the politically conscious Iranians against royal tyranny. The European experience had shown them that the remedy of absolutism lay in constitutionalism. This term summed up for them the ideals of self-government, nationalism and democracy. So they launched a movement to press the king to grant a constitution and convene a national assembly.

The first National Consultative Assembly convened after the Constitutional Revolution of 1906 was composed entirely of individuals and there was no sign of any political concerting. But during the term of the second Assembly a rudiment of a party system emerged. The members became split into a pro-government majority calling themselves *moderates* and an opposing minority calling themselves *democrats*. But these loose formations had no connection with political life outside parliament and were visible only during the sessions of the Assembly. With Reza Khan's coming to power in 1921 even these fleeting formations disappeared as there were no more strong personalities to lead them. Reza Khan banned all groups and political activity. As a result, no political party existed in Iran till his downfall in 1941.

In the relaxed atmosphere after the exile of Reza Khan a large number of political groups were formed but soon faded into obscurity. Out of these formations only one, the Tudah Party, has been acknowledged as the first modern broad-based political party with a centralized organization, leadership and cadres and a large network of front organizations. From the humble beginning in 1941 with 30,000 activists its strength rose by 1946 to 1,00,000 when it was outlawed by the pro-western monarch for its left-oriented ideology. It went underground, resurfaced during the revolutionary upheaval of 1978-79, collaborated with the "progressive" clergy who after consolidating their regime outlawed and liquidated the Tudeh along with all other non-clerical parties and groups in 1982.

Political Parties since 1979

Political groups that existed in Iran in the wake of Revolution of 1979 may be classified into following categories:

Marxist:

- * Tudeh Party; formed in 1941; banned in 1946; banned again in 1982.

Fidayeen-i-Islam

- * Islamo-Marxist group formed in 1963; in 1980 split between a majority faction which collaborated with the clergy; both were banned and liquidated in 1982.

Fidayeen-i-Khalq

- * Marxist-Leninist group founded in 1965; banned and liquidated in 1982.

Liberal-Islamic, non-clerical

* The National Front; founded in 1944; banned in 1982.
* The National Freedom Movement; founded in 1968; banned in 1982.

Radical-Islamic, non-clerical

* Mojahideen-i-Khalq; founded in 1965; banned in 1983.
* The Revolutionary Movement of the Muslim People of Iran; founded in 1978; banned in 1982.

Islamic-Clerical

* Association of the combatant Clergy of Tehran; founded in 1978.
* Organization of the Mojahideen of the Islamic Revolution; founded in 1979.
* Islamic Republican Party; founded in 1979; disbanded by the regime in 1987.

The political scene since 1987 is dominated by the conservative faction of the mujtahids. The alliance of moderate mujtahids with the reformist intellectuals, bureaucrats and technocrats was definitely trounced in the parliamentary election of 2004 and the presidential election of 2005.

In 1995 the Islamic Consultative Assembly had passed the Law on Political Parties, Associations, Unions and Clubs under which a licensing commission was appointed to vet applications for the formation of parties, associations and unions and grant them licence to operate publicly.[2] The conditions are stringent and only the pro-regime groups are allowed to function openly. Since then more than 80 groups were granted licences but there is still no trace of any party system. The guardian class appears to have supplanted the party system. If one faction sits in government the other group comes out in opposition. That explains the phenomenon of partyless oligarchy.

References

1. Cf. Ann K.S. Lambton. "Persian Political Societies 1906-11" in St. Antony's Papers, No. 16, edited by Albert Hourani (London : Chatoo & Windus, 1963).
2. *Ittela'at*, 1 June 1995.

9

Iran in World Affairs

The Origins of Iranian Foreign Policy

Foreign policy of a nation as the sum of principles guiding its conduct in world affairs is but a continuation of its domestic policy. The worldview and foreign policy of the Islamic Republic has been shaped by the experiences of the Safavid, Qajar and Pahlavi eras.

Persia was one of the great empires of the world during the Achaemenian era (546 BC-330) and the Sassanian era (226-641 AD). The Sassanid empire extended from the modern day Iraq to the modern day Afghanistan. Then Iran was conquered by the Arabs and integrated with the Arab empire. With the decline of Arab power Iran was spintered into a number of principalities. After a spell of Mongolian rule Iran again returned to chaos and fragmentation.

It was for Ismail Safavi, a Turkish chief of Shiite creed, to defeat his rivals with the help of Qizilbashes, a Turkoman tribe converted to Shiism, and declare himself as king of Persia at Ardbil in 1501. Immediately after declaring himself as king of Persia he declared Shiism as the official religion of his state and started converting his subjects to the state religion. The rationale for building an Iranian nationality on the basis of Shiism was that he wanted to preserve his kingdom's independence against the mighty Ottoman Empire in the west, ruled by Sunni sultans. Thus the foundation of modern Iran's foreign policy was laid on hatred of the Sunnis and the Ottomans and by default on friendship with Christian European powers who were the sworn enemies of Islam and the Ottomans. Ismail's sectarian approach towards the surrounding Muslim territories isolated the Iranians from the Muslim peoples. At the height of his power Persia's territory extended from Iraq to Afghanistan. But Ismail's policy of forcible conversions landed him in trouble with the Ottomans. The Turkish sultan declared Shiism as heresy and equated killing of one Shiite to killing of seventy infidels. This provoked the massacre of some 40,000 Shiites in Anatolia. In retaliation, Ismail got twice that number of Sunnites killed in Iran.[1] Ismail was also fond of meddling in Turkish affairs. When Ahmad, younger brother of Sultan Selim I, rebelled against him Ismail provided him aid and support. To punish Ismail the Turkish army invaded Iran. Historians tell about a historic battle fought between the Turkish and Persian armies at Chaldiran on 23 August 1514 which resulted in the killing of some 50,000 troops on each side and ended with the ignominious defeat of Persia and humbling of Ismail. This single event is stated to have created permanent hatred between the two sects and was responsible for isolating Iran from the Muslim world for centuries. The disgruntled Ismail then turned to European powers to seek their support against the Turks. The Europeans did nothing but to use Iran against the Turks to distract them from Europe.

The Safavid era came to an end in 1736 and was followed by Qajar rule. Early Qajars were powerful and ruled effectively but later Qajars became corrupt and degenerate. Their weakness became evident in 1805 when Russia invaded Georgia (then a province of Iran) and annexed it. Agitated by this event the mujtahids exhorted the king to declare war against Russia. The war ended in utter defeat for Persia and signing of the Treaty of Gulistan in 1806 by which Persia had to cede some territory to Russia as reparation. Another war fought with Russia ended in yet another defeat for Persia and signing of the Treaty of Turkomanchai in 1828 under which Persia ceded all its Trans-Caucasian territories to Russia. Then a weak Persia invited foreign incursion. Russia proceeded from the north to impose its imperialistic domination over Persia and Britain occupied the Persian Gulf region and tried to bring Persia under her control so that it could forestall any possible advance of any hostile power towards her Indian Empire. Thus Persia was caught in the rivalry between the two great empires. Eventually the two powers concluded the so-called Anglo-Russian Convention in 1908 by which Russia carved out its sphere of influence in the northern half and Britain carved out its sphere of influence in the southern half of Persia. Then oil was discovered by the British explorers in Iran. They obtained a long-term concession for oil exploration and extraction from the Persian government in lieu of a paltry royalty. Henceonwards the British government developed besides the strategic interest an economic ones also in Iran. The power game of the great powers in Iran, the Tobacco Rebellion 1890-92, the Constitutional Revolution of 1905-11; Reza Khan's dictatorship during 1921-41 with covert British support; the occupation of Iran by the Allies during World War II; the withdrawal of Western forces after the war but stay of Soviet forces in the north and installation of puppet communist governments in the Iranian provinces of Azerbaijan and Kurdistan; the overthrow of the Musaddeq government through a CIA-engineered *coup d' etat*; then Iran's alliance with the USA and Israel and penetration of foreign advisers and experts in large numbers and the growing pauperization of Iranians as a result of erring modernization drive of the Shah, all these and many other events left a deep imprint on the minds of Iranians and shaped their attitude towards the external world.

Until World War II Iran was a backward agrarian country. Its independent capitalist development was blocked because of the interplay of domestic feudal and foreign imperialist forces. Ever since the nineteenth century the economic history of Iran has been a history of ruthless exploitation, economic stagnation, scarcities, financial bankruptcy and mass poverty. Reza Khan was the first ruler who laid the foundation of modern industry in Iran but that process was halted by World War II. His successor Muhammad Reza became in due course an imperialist stooge and his faulty modernization drive was responsible for widening the rich-poor gap, increasing income disparities and producing mass misery and destitution.

Since World War II exports of oil and gas have been the mainstay of the Iranian economy. Oil revenues finance about 80 per cent of the national budget. Thus Iran is a rentier state where an affluent minority thrives on state revenues while the larger majority ekks out a miserable existence. The devastation caused by the Iran-Iraq War of 1980-88, dwindling revenue from oil and gas, and depletion of these natural resources has convinced the Iranians of the need to develop their non-oil economy by rapid industrialization, agricultural development and import substitution to achieve national self-reliance. These concerns were reflected in the four national development plans launched so far by the clerical regime. Since a strong economy is the base for an independent foreign policy and national defence Iranian foreign policy has an important economic content and utmost emphasis has been placed on diversifying and developing foreign economic relations.[2]

Foreign Relations during the Pahlavi Era

From the mid-nineteenth century till the end of World War I the general condition of Iran was that of economic stagnation, military vulnerability and political dependence upon great powers. In February 1921 the USSR forced Persia to sign a treaty of friendship under which Russia obtained the right to station her troops on the Iranian soil if she was threatened of invasion by a third power through Iran. In 1979 the clerical regime abrogated the clause of the treaty which permitted stationing of Russian troops in Iran. On assuming power in 1921 the first priority of Reza Khan was the restoration of national honour and dignity by abrogating all unequal treaties and ending extra-territorial rights granted to foreigners. In 1932 he terminated the oil concession granted to d'Arcy, a British National, in 1901 but under pressure from the British government restored it. In 1937 he signed the so-called Saadabad Pact with Turkey, Iraq and Afghanistan for regional security. During World War II Reza Khan was believed to have approached Nazi Germany for German aid and technical assistance for Iran's economic development. For this he lost his throne in 1941 and was exiled to South Africa. The Allies occupied Iran jointly to keep their supply route open during the war. The western forces withdrew in 1945 and the Russians in 1946.

When Muhammad Reza ascended the throne in 1941 the country was suffering massively from the consequences of the war and was in utter chaos. In 1950 the nationalists government headed by Muhammad Musaddeq decided to nationalize the Iranian oil industry hoping to augment oil revenues and work for national development. Later developments proved that the king of Iran had become a stooge of Western powers and was hell bent on crushing his own people to subserve Western interests. In foreign affairs too he was an ally and camp-follower of the Western bloc. In 1950 Iran was the first Muslim country to recognize Israel and develop contacts with it. In 1953 he signed the Baghdad Pact of collective self-defence with Turkey, Iraq and Britain.

Emboldened by the oil wealth and western support the Shah followed an imperialist policy in the neighbouring Persian Gulf region. He laid a claim to Bahrain, Hirmand and Shatt al Arab. The Bahrainians decided for independence in a referendum organized by the United Nations in 1971. After British withdrawal from the Gulf region Iranian troops occupied the three Arab-inhabited islands of Abu Musa, Little Tumb and Greater Tumb, located in the Strait of Hormuz. In 1975 Iran forced Iraq to sign an agreement to settle the Iran-Iraq border midway of Shatt al-Arab river.

Foreign Relations of the Islamic Republic

The objectives of foreign policy of the Islamic Republic have been defined under Article 152 of the 1979 Constitution as "Negation of all types of hegemonism, preservation of absolute independence and territorial integrity of the state, defence of the rights of all Muslims, non-alignment in relation to the imperialist powers, and peaceful relations with all non-enemy states.[3]

The above appears to be an idealistic formulation of Iran's foreign policy goals. Iran has not lagged behind other great nations who set their national goals in moralistic terms. The clerical state no doubt started as a revolutionary regime dedicated to a revolutionary ideology and brandishing a revolutionary blueprint in foreign affairs. The ideological zeal and radical rhetoric persisted so long as Khomeini lived. In the flush of their victory the hawkish mujtahids spoke of exporting their revolution to the surrounding Islamic lands. But underneath this veneer there appears to be a remarkable continuity of power-political and strategic objectives. The high mujtahids did not say that they will vacate the three Arab islands in the Gulf which were forcibly occupied by Muhammad Reza but acting like his disciples they declared that the occupied islands were an integral part of Iran and they will fight to the finish to retain them under their sovereignty. Iranian nationalism was displayed in full force during the long drawn Iraq-Iran War. After Khomeini's death the ideological fervour evaporated entirely. His successors are not a radical revolutionary but state-oriented conservative force dedicated to the pursuit of nationalistic goals. The core concept of Iranian academic discourse is Iran's national interests rather than radical Shiism. The most important feature of Iranian foreign policy since 1989 is its deradicalization and a growing realization of the need of ending Iran's isolation from the Arab-Islamic world and the rest of the international community, accerlerating the pace of economic development and building military might, including a nuclear potential, to withstand the pressures of hostile powers.

Clerical Iran's pragmatism is visible nowhere more than in its approach to the Arab-Islamic world. For centuries Iranian foreign policy was governed by hatred of the Sunnite world. Even as late as in khomeinmi's last phase the Saudis were denounced as being "American lackeys" and their Islam was branded as "American Islam". Khomeini never spoke kindly of the Arab sheikhdoms. Diplomatic relations with Saudi Arabia were broken in 1988 in the wake of killing of some Iranian pilgrims at the hands of Saudi Police for raising slogans against the "Great Satan" [the USA] and Israel during the *hajj* (annual pilgrimage) of 1987 in Mecca.

But after the end of Iraq-Iran War Khomeini's successors wholeheartedly sought friendship and co-operation with the Arab world. Diplomatic relations with Saudi Arabia were restored in 1991. But cordial relations were not resumed until Akbar Hashemi Rafsanjani, a veteran mujtahid and a former President of the Republic, went to Mecca to perform *umra* (optional pilgrimage to Mecca) in 1998 and utilized this occasion to meet and conciliate the Saudi leadership.

Iran's relations with Egypt go back to ancient times. Muhammad Reza was staunchly opposed to Jamal Abdul Nasir and his Arab nationalist policy. But when he was succeeded by the pro-West Anwar El-Sadat the Shah honoured him and treated him as a brother. In 1979 the clerical regime broke diplomatic relations with Egypt apparently for her signing the peace treaty with Israel but the real grievance was against Egypt's granting of diplomatic asylum to the deposed Shah of Iran (who died of cancer in Cairo on 27 July 1980). Diplomatic relations with Egypt were restored in February 2004.

Iran's relations with the Persian Gulf emirates have had a chequered history. Iran draws a lot of economic benefit from the UAE markets but the territorial dispute over the three occupied Arab islands lingers on. The Islamic Consultative Assembly on 20 April 1993 passed a law extending Iran's territorial waters to a limit which encloses the three disputed islands of Abu Musa, Greater Tumb and Lesser Tumb. In retaliation the Gulf Cooperation Council (GCC) on 8 June 1993 reaffirmed the sovereignty of the UAE over the islands. The dispute has, however, not hindered Iran's lucrative trade with the UAE and Dubai re-exports to Iran the much needed goods which partially offsets the American trade embargo against Iran.

Syria and Lebanon are the only Arab countries with which Iran has had consistently good relations because one is ruled by an anti-Sunni elite and the other has a sizeable Shii population.

In pursuit of this pro-Arab policy, Iranian statesmen and trade delegations paid frequent visits to Arab capitals during the 1990's and Iran secured on 1 December 2003 the status of an observer at the League of the Arab States and has expressed her desire to become a full member of the Gulf Cooperation Council (GCC).

The change in Iranian foreign policy is no more visible than in its approach towards the Muslim world. Iranian mujtahids have fully realized the potential of their Islamic connection. So gone are the days of "political" or "radical" Islam. They also conceal the sectarian nature of their state and their sectarian exclusivism. From the very beginning Khomeini and his followers have advocated Islamic unity against western imperialism. Iran's membership in the 57 nation Organization of the Islamic Conference (OIC) is a major departure from Iran's Shiite past.[4] The regime celebrates the first week of the third lunar month of the Islamic calendar as the "Islamic Unity Week" and each year an International Conference on Islamic Unity is convenedin Tehran. But notwithstanding this new found love for the Islamicic community Iran's special connection with Shiite communities continues.

Iran's relations with the great powers occupy a special place in Iranian diplomacy. Since the collapse of the USSR Iran has deepened its commercial, economic and strategic relationship with Russia. In 1985 a joint economic commission was established. In 1989 Iran signed an agreement with the USSR for cooperation in peaceful use of nuclear energy.

In 1995 Iran signed another agreement with Russia for the completion of a 1,300 megawatt nuclear reactor at Bushehr in the south of Iran which was started by the royal regime in 1975 but was abandoned by the German contractor in 1979. In the same year Russia agreed to supply two light water reactors for commissioning at Bushehr. The supply of Russian weapons and military hardware was resumed in 2001 in defiance of American-imposed trade embargo against Iran.

For three decades Iran was an ally and protectorate of the USA. Iranian mujtahids who had turned against their Shah had also turned against his protector and overlord. Iran's connection with the USA was suddenly rupturned on 4 November 1979 when a group of pro-Khomeini students stormed the American Embassy in Tehran and took about 65 American diplomatic workers as hostages. Although the hostages were released on 20 January 1981 the episode deeply injured the American psyche. The hostage-taking drama is believed to have been played under the impact of two isolated events: *First*, a few days earlier Prime Minister of the Provisional Government of Iran Mahdi Bazargan and his Foreign Minister Ibrahim Yazdi had met with American National Security Adviser Zbigniew Brzezinski in Algiers (Algeria) where the two leaders had gone to attend an Afro-Asian conference. The meeting had taken place without Khomeini's knowledge. This aroused the fear and apprehension about a possible American plot against the revolutionary regime in the style of 1953.[5] *Second*, the Carter Administration had allowed the exiled Shah to enter a New York hospital for the treatment of his cancer. The mujtahids felt that the USA might grant him diplomatic asylum and use him against Iran. So they demanded his repatriation before the American hostages were released.

Iran on 5 November 1979 abrogated the Mutual Defence Assistance Agreement signed with the USA in 1959. In retaliation the USA stopped the imports of Iranian oil and froze Iranian assets held in American banks. On 7 April 1980 the US broke diplomatic relations with Iran and banned all American exports to Iran. In 1993 the American Administration charged Iran of developing weapons of mass destruction which was denied by Iran. On 30 April 1995 the Clinton Administration issued an executive order imposing a total ban on all trade with and investment in Iran, including purchases of Iranian oil. In 1996 the executive order was replaced by the Iran and Libya Sanctions Act imposing secondary sanctions against foreign companies investing an amount of US$ 40 million or more annually in Iran. The act was further renewed in 2000 for a period of five years. Sanctions against Libya were lifted in 2004. In July 2001 the USA vetoed Iran's bid to enter the World Trade Organization (WTO) and again in 2002. In

2002 and 2003 Americans objected to Iran's nuclear research programme alleging that it was directed towards military use. In 2003 President George W. Bush branded Iran as an "axis of evil" along with North Korea and Iraq. After succeeding in toppling the Saddam Hussain regime and occupying Iraq the Bush Administration was emboldened to apply extreme pressure on Iran. The Americans now started accusing openly that Iran's nuclear programme was directed at making nuclear weapons and demanded that Iran give up its nuclear programme. During 2004 and 2005 the European allies of the USA applied intense diplomatic pressure against Iran for termination of its nuclear programme. The matter was raised before the International Atomic Energy Agency (IAEA) which imposed a tough inspections regime on Iran's nuclear facilities. American lobbying was instrumental in IAEA's September 2005 resolution which threatened to refer Iran's case to the UN Security Council and on 4 February 2006 actually referred it to the Security Council and threatened to recommend the imposition of sanctions.

Although a via media was being searched to defuse the crisis and save Iran from imposition of possible sanctions by putting the Iranian nuclear programme under the tutelage of Russia which could then restrain it from developing nuclear weapons in view of deep-rooted American enemity with Iran the matter is not expected to stop there. America is likely to pursue a policy of isolating Iran from the International community, undermining its credibility, and toppling its regime.

Iran's relations with Europe have seen many ups and downs since 1979. Relations were bedevilled in the first decade of the Iranian Revolution, particularly over

Khomeini's *fatwa* regarding Salman Rushdie's blasphemy against the Prophet Muhammad and his family. A compromise was reached between Iranian and European leaders in 1998 whereby Iran undertook not to execute Khomeini's *fatwa* against Rushdie and the Europeans agreed to restore diplomatic relations with Iran and end its political and economic boycott. The interest of the European Union in Iran is confined to its oil and gas and as a market for European goods and commodities.

As regards the rest of the world Iran has developed a special relationship with its central Asian neighbours and China, India, North and South Korea and Japan. She joined the Economic Cooperation Organization (ECO) in 1990.

References

1. Rene Grossets, *La face de l' Asie* (Paris: Payot, 1962), pp. 112 ff., as cited by Jalal A'l-i-Ahmad, *Gharbzedgi* (Tehran, 1964), p. 69.
2. Cf. Ruhullah K. Ramzani, *The Foreign Policy of Iran.* A Developing Nation in World Affairs, 1500-1941 (Charlottesville: University of Virginia Press, 1966); Shahram Chubin and Sepehr Zabih, *The Foreign Relations of Iran* (Berkeley: University of California Press, 1975); and George Lenczowski, *Russia and the West in Iran* (Ithaca: Cornell University Press, 1949).
3. Shireen T. Hunter, *Iran and the World* (Bloomington: Indiana University Press, 1990).
4. Tehran hosted the eighth conference of the heads of states or government of the Organizaion of the Islamic Conference (OIC) on 9-11 October 1997.
5. Z.K. Brzezinski, *Power and Principle.* Memoirs of a National Security Adviser, 1977-1981 (New York: Farrar, Strauss & Giroux, 1983).

Conclusion

This study started with a survey of the principal political events and developments in Iran during the period 1900-1979 to explain the factors and forces that led to the Revolution of 1979 and the emergence of the Islamic Republic. Within the span of a century Iran witnessed two revolutions one a non-violent liberal-constitutional and the other a violent one. The first ushered in constitutional rule. The experiment failed because of deep-routed tradition of authoritarianism and the abject poverty and ignorance of the masses and the intrigues of foreign powers. The seeds of the second revolution were hidden in the excesses and atrocities of the post-constitutional era. Although the revolution of 1979 was a popular revolution brought about by the joint struggle of the Iranian masses including the religious class and the revolutionary forces of both the left and right it did not lead to freedom and democracy because when the tyrannical regime collapsed the democratic forces faultered so the religious class took the lead and captured state power.

The constitution of the Islamic Republic institutionalizes the ideas and ideals of the guardian class of radical mujtahids regarding individual freedom, authority, leadership and political obligation. The Islamic Republic is in no sense a democratic republic: it does not even peretend to be a democracy; it is at best a plebiscitary dictatorship. The mujtahids have outrightly discarded all western notions of liberalism, constitutionalism and democracy. There is nothing novel in this patrimonial system. It is merely another variety of Middle Eastern despotism.

The bedrock of this authoritarian regime is the cardinal principle of *Vilayat-i-faqih* (custodianship of the jurisconsult) which institutionalizes and entrenches the monopolistic, monolithic and omnipotent, omnicompetent and omnipresent rule of the guardian class. The *valiyy-i-faqih* (the custodian jurist) is the representative and leader of the guardian class who claims on their bealf to be the living counterpart of the Hidden Imam and repository of his spiritual and temporal authority. In that capacity he is the supreme leader of the system and source of all authority and legitimacy. He is the summit of the political system and the topmost rung of the power-structure. The power rungs of *Pasdaran-i-Inquilab* (Revolutionary Guards), the armed forces, the police force, the bureaucracy, the Assembly of Experts on Leadership, the Islamic Consultative Assembly, the President of the Republic and the judicial authorities are all auxiliaries of clerical power and sustain clerical hegemony.

The system is authoritarian in nature and totalitarian in its sweep because it recognizes no freedoms and rights against the state, acknowledges no limits to state authority, outlaws all dissent and opposition and imposes ideological uniformity and conformism upon the society.

A universal feature of western democracies is that political life is organized and government and parliament are run by broad-based political parties organized on the basis of policies and programmes. In Iran, because of stunted political development, a viable democratic party system could not come into being. The clerical regime had by 1983 annihilated all non-clerical parties and groups of both the left and right. The only instrument of political mobilization created by the mujtahids in 1979 *Hizb-i-Jumhuriyy-i-Islami* (The Islamic Republican Party) was disbanded by the clerical establishment because they were not prepared to empower the progeny of the plebian class and share political power with them (May Allah forgive me for this blasphemy, Amen !)

The absence of a party system explains the peculiar phenomenon of class supplanting the party as an organizer of political life. The clerical establishment may be split into factions and the regime may license its loyalists tô form associations and parties none cannot match the class as an organizing political force.

Is there any prospects of change in this fixed, rigid and static power structure? The answer is that there are no signs of any transformation in the immediate future, nor is the future course of political development predictable. But by way of political speculation at least four scenarios may be visualized: *first*, a regime change through foreign military intervention; *second*, a regime change through a *coup d' etat* which is unlikely in view of the categorical loyalty of the armed forces to the regime; *third*, a transformation as a result of intra-regime shifting of balance of forces but that is impossible. The events of 2004 and 2005 have shown how the conservatives outsmarted the moderates and emasculated them; and *fourth*, evolutionary transformation through generational change. It is most likely that the old guard will pass away in another 25 years and their mantle will be assumed by a new generation of leaders who may chart out a new course.

Appendix A

The Constitution of the Islamic Republic of Iran*

The Preamble

The Fundamental Law [or the constitution] of the Islamic Republic of Iran which shapes the cultural, social, political and economic institutions of the Iranian society according to Islamic principles and ordinances reflects the heart-felt aspirations of the Islamic nation. The struggle of the Muslim people from the beginning till the victory as expressed through the categorical and devastating slogans raised by all strata of the population articulated this basic aspiration and now at the dawn of the victory our great nation desires the realization of this aspiration.

The uniqueness of the present Revolution, as compared with the other Iranian movements of the past century, lies in its ideological and Islamic character. From the Constitutional Movement against despotism and the anti-colonial movement for the nationalization of oil the Muslim nation has gained

* *Translated from Persian– The text includes the constitutional achievements of 1989.*

this valuable experience that the root cause and indicator of the failure of these movements was their non-ideological character. Although these movements were influenced by Islamic ideals and the combatant clergy had taken a leading part in them these movements faded out because these struggles were removed from the pure Islamic ideals. From now on the awakened conscience of the nation under the leadership of the exalted Source of Emulation the Greatest Symbol of God Imam Khomeini discovered the need to follow the pure line of the Islamic ideological movement and this time the struggling clergy which was always in the forefront of the popular movements in association with the committed writers and intellectuals under their leadership found a new dynamism. The last movement of the Iranian nation started in 1382 Hijri lunar or 1341 Hijri solar [corresponding to 1962 AD].

The Vanguard of the Movement

The dnmevastating protest of Imam Khomeini against the American inspired "White Revolution" which was a step towards reinforcing the foundations of the despotic regime and consolidating the political, cultural and economic dependence of Iran upon world imperialism, became the impetus for launching the monolithic movement of the nation and in the wake of that great and bloody uprising of the Islamic community in the month of *Khordad* 1343 HS [corresponding to June 1963 AD] that really triggered this glorious and mass uprising, confirmed and consolidated the central position of the Imam as an Islamic Leader. Despite Imam's exile from the country in the wake of his protest against the shameful law of the capitulations [immunity of

American advisers from local legal jurisdiction] the strong attachment of the community with the Imam continued and the Muslim community, particularly the committed intellectuals and the combatant clergy, carried on their activities amidst exile, imprisonment, torture and executions.

Meanwhile, the conscious and responsible strata of the society started soul-searching in the strongholds of the mosques, the seminaries and the universities and inspired by the revolutionary ideology of Islam started raising the ideological and revolutionary of the suppression of the Islamic movement by launching violent attacks on the Madrasa Faiziyya, the universities and other centres of revolutionary activity tried to put down the revolutionary anger of the people. Meanwhile, the execution squads, torturing in the medieval style and long-term sentences was the price our nation paid for its firm determination to continue the struggle. The blood of hundreds of young believing men and women who while raising the cry of "*Allah-O-Akbar*" at dawn in the streets and those who fell victim to the bullets of the enemy in the lanes and bazaars contributed to the continuity of the Islamic Revolution of Iran. The recurrent statements and messages of the Imam on various occasions and endowed ever increasing depth and breadth to the consciousness and determination of the Islamic community.

Islamic Government

The pattern of Islamic government based on the *Vilayat-i-faqih* (of the jurisconsult) shown to the Muslim people at the height of the convulsions of the despotic regime gave them a specific and new systematic cause to work for and opened the way for the genuine ideological struggle of Islam which consolidated the efforts of the committed Muslim combatants at home and abroad.

The movement continued on this line until popular dissatisfaction and ever increasing anger of the people in the face of ever increasing suppression and repression at home and the revelations regarding these events and representation of the struggle at the world level by the clergy and the struggling students shook the foundations of the authority of the regime and the regime and it overlords were forced to lessen the repression and choking and attempted to open up the political atmosphere in the country so that according to their assumption by opening a window or pacify the people they could forestall the final collapse of the regime

However, the restive, conscious and determined nation under the resolute and unshakeable leadership of the Imam continued their successful and united uprising throughout the country.

The Anger of the Nation

The publication of a defamatory letter (in the official newspapers) on 17 Dey 1356 HS (7 January 1978) on behalf of the authorities that was derogatory to the venerable status of the clergy in general and Imam Khomeini in particular, accelerated the pace of the movement and unleashed the anger of the people throughout the country. To control this volcanic eruption of the people's anger the regime tried to silence it by fire and blood. Instead this very attempt circulated more blood in the veins of the Revolution. The heat-wave of the Revolution persisted through the weekly and fortieth day commemorations of the martyrdom of the martyrs of the Revolution and imparted life, warmth and ever-increasing resurgence to the movement, throughout the country and with a view to continue the popular uprising all the organizations went on total strike and all the people actively participated in street demonstrations to bring about the collapse of the despotic regime. The participation of men and women of all strata of the society and of all religions and political persuasions was significantly a determining factor in this struggle. Especially the women were conspicuous ay their active presence everywhere at all stages of this great jihad. Such sights as a mother with her child in the lap running towards the field of action facing gun-barrels were indicative of the large and decisive role played ay this great stratum of the society in the struggle.

The Price that the Nation Paid

The sapling of the revolution came to fruition after continuous and persistent struggle over a year or so with the blood of sixty thousand martyrs and one hundred thousand wounded or disabled and material losses of billions of *tumans*, amidst cries of "Independence, Freedom, Islamic Government". This great movement relying on faith, unity and decisive leadership at the critical and explosive stages and with the sacrifices of the nation became victorious and smashed all imperialist calculations, connections and organs. By its nature it became a new chapter in the popular revolutions of the world.

21 and 22 *Bahman* 1357 HS (corresponding to 10 and 11 collapse February 1979) were the days of the imperialist foundation and internal despotism and external domination dependent on it. With this victory

the vanguard of the Islamic government that is the long-cherished aspiration of the Muslim people gave the good new of final victory.

The Iranian nation as a whole and with the participation of the sources of emulation and the Islamic scholars and the Supreme Leader in the referendum on the Islamic Republic gave their final and categorical opinion in favour of the creation of a new system of Islamic Republic and approved it by a majority of 98.2 per cent votes.

Now the Fundamental Law of the Islamic Republic as an explicator of institutions and political, social, culture and economic relations in the society must open the way of strengthening the bases of Islamic government and guide the construction of a new system of government on the ruins of the former tyrannical system.

Government under Islam

From the Islamic viewpoint government is not a product of a class system or the domination of an individual or groups. Rather it is an expression of the political ideals of a nation united in belief and thought which creates the necessary structures so that in the process of ideological and religious transformation it may open its way towards the final goal (movement towards God). Our nation in the course of its revolutionary perfection has washed off all dust and rust of the unjust system, purified itself all mixtures of alien ideologies and has returned to the pure and pristine ideals and world-view of Islam and is now determined to build a model society according to Islamic standards. On that basis the mission of Fundamental Law is to accord an ideal character to the spiritual foundations of the Movement and to create conditions under which human beings could develop their personalities in accordance with the noble and universal values of Islam.

The Fundamental Law in respect of the substance of the Islamic Revolution of Iran which is a movement for the victory of the poor and oppressed over the oppressors and the arrogant provides a ground for the perpetuation of this Revolution at home and abroad. Particularly, by expanding international relations with other Islamic movements and peoples it strive to pave the way for the creation of a single world Islamic community ("Verily, this community of yours is one community and I am your creator so worship me") so that the struggle for liberation of the deprived and oppressed people throughout the world finds strength.

In view of the character of this great movement, the Fundamental Law shall guarantee the negation of all kinds of intellectual and social authoritarianism and economic monopolism so that the people become the masters of their own destines ("He releases them from heavy burden and the yokes which were upon them").

In the creation of organs and political structures that are themselves the basis of the social structure, the Virtuous, on the basis of their ideological perfection, shall take the charge of government and administration ("Verily, my virtuous slaves shall inherit the earth") and law-making that lays down rules for social management must proceed on the basis of the Quran and the *sunnah*. In this ground the close and serious supervision (over the governance) on the part just, pious and Islamist scholars (just jurists is an indispensable necessity. Because the objective of government is to prepare man for movement towards God ("And to God is the eventual return") so that the ground for the genesis and growth of God-like qualities in man is prepared ("Adopt the code of conduct of God") and this is not possible except by the participation of all elements of the society in the process of the transformation of the society.

In regard to this aspect, the Fundamental Law provides the necessary opportunities for such participation at all the levels of political decision-making and determination of their destines by all individuals in the society so that in the course of self-perfection every man becomes his own ruler and accountable unto himself for his growth, evolution and self-guidance. This will be the very realization of the government of the weak upon earth ("And we intend to do favour to those who were oppressed upon earth and We shall make them the leaders and We shall make them the inheritors").

Guardianship of the Just *Faqih*

On the basis of the continuous guardianship and leadership of the community the Fundamental Law prepares the ground for the identification of an all perfect *Faqih* who is acknowledged by the people as their leader. "The *ulama* are administrators of affairs who are appointed by God to keep the boundaries of *Halaal* (permitted) and the *Haraam* (forbidden) so that they could guarantee that no organization deviates from the performance of its allotted Islamic functions.

The Economy is a Means, Not an End

In the strengthening of the foundations of the economy the principle is the fulfillment of the basis needs of the people in the course of their growth and self-perfection and not like other economic systems the concentration of wealth and accumulation and profit-seeing. Because in the materialist school the economy is an end in itself and from this view in the course of growth the economy becomes a destructive and corrupting factor. But in Islam the economy is a means which could only be utilized for the best attainment of the goals.

From this perspective the Islamic economic programme aims at creating the proper grounds for promoting the unequal creative capabilities and provision of work for all and fulfillment of the basic needs of the people necessary for their continuous growth is the responsibility of the Islamic government.

Women under the Constitution

In the creation of Islamic social structures, human resources which hitherto have been in the service all-round foreign exploitation shall recover their real identity and their human rights. In this recovery it is but natural that the women who have borne the most the oppression of the former tyrannous system should enjoy their rights more. The family is the basis unit of the society and the real frame for the growth and excellence or man. The compatibility of beliefs and ideals in the formation of the family is the real condition of the growth and self-perfection of man and provisions of opportunities towards the realization of this objective is the responsibility of the Islamic government. Woman in this framework of family is freed from being "some object" or being an "instrument" in the service of promotion of consumerism and exploitation and by regaining her important function of motherhood in the preparation of civilised individuals will be the forerunner and co-worker with the menfolk in all walks of human activity and in the end shall be the bearer of greater responsibility and from the Islamic perspective shall enjoy greater value and dignity.

The Committed Military

In organising and equipping the country's defence forces attention should be paid to the fact that faith and ideology should be the basis and the rule. For this army of the Islamic Republic and the Corps of the Revolutionary Guards shall be organised in accordance with the above goal and shall not only protect and guard the borders but shall also be responsible to carry the ideological mission of *Jihad* (struggle) in the way of God and expansion of rule of divine law in the world. ("And prepare for them whatever you could, including steeds of war, to strike terror into the hearts of the enemies of God and your enemies, and others besides them.")

Justice under the Constitution

The question of justice in respect of safeguarding the rights of the people on the lines of the Islamic movement and to prevent deviations from the norms within the Islamic community is a vital matter. From this point installation of a judicial system on the basis of Islamic justice and composed of just judges well-acquainted with minute religious rules has been provided for. Because ideologically committed the system is infused with fundamental sensitivity and care so it is essential that it be kept away from all sorts of unsound contacts and connections ("And when you adjudicate between people adjudicate with equity").

The Executive Power

The executive branch by virtue of the special importance that it possesses in relation to the enforcement of the Islamic rules and ordinances to maintain just relations in the society and likewise in view of the need to prepare the ground for attaining the ultimate goals of life, must open the way for the establishment of an Islamic society. Consequently any system that because of its complexities makes access to this goals difficult must be nullified. With this objective the bureaucratic system that is a product of the *taghuti* (authoritarian) rule will be strongly rejected so that the executive system is able to fulfill its administrative duties with as much speed as possible.

The Media of Mass Communication

The mass media (radio, television, etc.) should be dedicated towards propagation of the Islamic culture to complete the evolutionary course of the Islamic Revolution. In this respect they should take benefit from the healthy and sound thoughts and must desist from propagating destructive and anti-Islamic tendencies.

Compliance with the principles of such law that has the freedom and dignity of the humankind in the forefront of its objectives and opens the way of growth and perfection of man is the responsibility of all. It is essential that the Muslim community by selecting expert and believing functionaries and by continues supervision over their functioning should participate in the building of an Islamic society with the hope that in the structure of a model Islamic society they become successful in presenting an exemplary model to all the people of the world ("And like that we made you a community of the middle path so that you could become witnesses to people.")

The Representatives

The Assembly of Experts (*Majlis-i-Khobregan*) composed of the representatives of the people finalized the codification of this Constitution, on the basis of deliberation over the draft presented by the government and various proposals received from the different sections of the people, into twelve chapters comprising one hundred seventy-five articles [the total number of articles increased to 177 as a result of amendments of 1989], at the threshold of the fifteenth century of the Hijra [migration of the Prophet from Mecca to Medina] with the above objectives and aspirations, in the hope that this century shall be the century of rule of all the weak people of the world and destruction of rule of the arrogant mighty.

Chapter I

General Principles

Article 1

The government of Iran is an Islamic Republic that the Iranian nation on the basis of their deep belief in just rule and Quranic justice and in the wake of the victorious Islamic Revolution of theirs under the leadership of the exalted source of emulation the Greatest Symbol of God, Imam Khomeini, in a referendum held on 10 and 11 Farvardin 1358 HS corresponding to 1 and 2 Jomadal oula 1399 HL [30-31 March 1979] by a majority of 98.2 per cent of the eligible voters voted in its favour.

Article 2

The Islamic Republic is a system based on belief in:

1. One and only God (*La Ilaha Illallah*) who is the sole source of authority and law and submission to whose commands is obligatory.
2. Divine revelation and its basic role in the formulation of laws.
3. The Day of Judgment (*Ma'ad*) and its constructive role in the evolutionary course leading mankind towards God.
4. Divine justice among people and legislation.
5. Continuous *Imamat* and leadership and its role in the continuity of the Islamic Revolution.
6. Man's dignity, high worth and freedom, coupled with his responsibility before God.

(a) continuous *ijtihad* by the qualified *fuqaha* (jurists) on the basis of the Holy Book and traditions of the Holy Imams;

(b) utilization of science, technology and all past human experiences and the quest for their further advancement;

(c) negation of all kinds of tyranny and oppression shall ensure justice and equity, political, economic, social and cultural independence and national solidarity.

Article 3

With a view to attaining the objectives mentioned under Article 2 the government of the Islamic

Republic is bound to use all its potentialities for the following tasks:

1. Creation of an environment favourable to the growth of moral qualities on the basis of faith, piety and fight against all manifestations of corruption and degradation.

2. Raising the level of awareness of the public in all spheres by proper utilization of the press, the mass media and other resources.

3. Free education, upkeep and physical training for all at all the levels and making higher education easy and accessible to all.

4. Revitalizing the spirit of research, assimilation and creativity in all scientific, technological, cultural and Islamic spheres by way of foundation of research centres and encouragement of researchers.

5. Complete elimination of colonialism and prevention of the influence of the foreigners.

6. Extermination of all types of autocracy, despotism and monopolism.

7. Guarantee of political and social freedoms within the limits of law.

8. General participation of people in the determination of their political, economic, social and cultural destiny.

9. Removal of unfair discrimination and creation of fair opportunities for all in all material and intellectual spheres.

10. Creation of a sound administrative system and abolition of all unnecessary structures.

11. Absolute strengthening of the foundations of national defence by the way of public military training for safeguarding national independence, territorial integrity and the Islamic order of the country.

12. Building up a sound and equitable economy for general well-being and alleviation of poverty and elimination of deprivation in all spheres of nutrition, housing, work, healthcare and social security.

13. Ensuring self-reliance in science and technology pertaining to industry, agriculture, military affairs and the like.

14. Guarantee of all rights of individuals men and women and provision of legal justice for all and equality of all before the law.

15. Development and strengthening of Islamic brotherhood and general cooperation among all the people.

16. Formulation of policy of the country on the basis of Islamic norms, brotherly commitment towards all Muslims and relentless support to the downtrodden of the world.

Article 4

All civil, criminal, financial, economic, administrative, cultural, military, political and other laws rules and regulations must conform with the

Islamic norms. This principle governs all the provisions of the fundamental Law and other laws and regulations. Determination of this matter (conformity of laws with Islamic norms) is the duty of the *fuqaha* (religious jurists) of the Guardian Council.

Article 5 (amended in 1989)

In the Islamic Republic of Iran the affairs of the country are administered by reliance on the public opinion as expressed through elections—election of the President of the Republic, of the Representatives of the Islamic Consultative Assembly of members of other consultative councils and the like; or by way of referendum on matters as provided for under other Articles of this Constitution.

Article 7

According to the Quranic ordinance: "And their governance is by *shura* mutual consultation" and "Consult them in matters of governance", the consultative councils, the Islamic Consultative Assembly, the consultative councils of the provinces, towns, cities, localities, districts, villages and the like are the pillars of decision taking and administration of the country.

The subjects, the structure, jurisdiction and functions of these consultative councils are decided by this Law and other laws flowing from it.

Article 8

In the Islamic Republic of Iran call to good deeds *(khair)*, exhorting to do what is proper *(Amr-bil-Maroof)* and dissuading from doing what is reprehensible *(Nihyi-an-al Munkar)* is a public obligation of all people in relation to each other, of the state in relation to the people and of people in relation the state. The conditions, limits and manner of these are determined by law. ("The believing men and the believing women are each other's caretakers. They enjoin what is proper and forbid what is reprehensible.")

Article 9

In the Islamic Republic freedom, independence, unity and territorial integrity of the country are inseparable from each other and their protection is a duty of the state and members of the nation. No individual or group or functionary has a right in the name of freedom to inflict any harm to the political, cultural, economic and military independence and territorial integrity of Iran and no functionary has a right in the name of protection of national independence and territorial integrity of the country to deprive the people of their just freedoms by means of laws and regulations.

Article 10

Whereas the family is the unit of the Islamic society all laws, regulations and planning connected therewith should aim at facilitating the formation of the family, maintain its sanctity and regulate family relations on the basis of Islamic laws and ethics.

Article 11

In accordance with the Quranic verse: "Verily this community of yours is one community and I am your Creator so worship me" all Muslims form a single community and the government of the Islamic Republic is duty-bound to formulate its general policies on the basis of solidarity and unity of Muslim nations and must exert consistent effort to realize the political, economic and cultural unity of the world of Islam.

Article 12

The official religion of Iran is Islam and the denomination is the Jafari *Ithana Ashari* [twelver Shiism] and this status is irrevocable for all enternity. Other denomination in general, i.e., the Hanafi, Shafe'I, Maliki, Hanbali, and Zaidi will enjoy full respect and the followers of these schools are free to perform their religious rites in accordance with their own jurisprudence and in respect of religious instruction and religious training and personal affairs (marriage divorce, inheritance and testament) and claims connected with them are recognized by the courts of law. Moreover, if in any region of the country the followers of any one these schools are in a majority local regulations with in the jurisdiction of the concerned local consultative councils shall be in accordance with that school subject to the protection of the rights of the followers of all other schools.

Article 13

Iranians of the Zorostrian, Jewish and Christian faiths alone are recognized as religious minorities. They are free to perform their religious rites within the limits of the law and in respect of their personal affairs and religious instruction act in accordance with their own religion.

Article 14

In accordance with the Quranic verse "Allah does not forbid you from giving fair treatment and doing justice to those who did not fight against you in matters of religion and did not expel you from your lands. Allah does love the justice-doers," the government of the Islamic Republic and the Muslims are duty-bound to deal with them with utmost courtesy and Islamic justice and take into consideration their human rights. This principle is valid only in respect of those who do not conspire or act against Islam or the Islamic Republic of Iran.

Chapter II

The Language, Script, Calendar and Flag of the Country

Article 15

The official and common language and script of the people of Iran is is Farsi (Persian).All documents, correspondence, official texts and textbooks should be in this language and script. But use of the local dialects and nationality languages in the press and the mass media and teaching of their literature along with Persian language is allowed.

Article 16

Whereas the language of Quran and the Islamic sciences and literature is Arabic and the Persian literature is completely commingled with this language it is desirable that this language by taught from the primary till the end of the secondary level in all classes and in all streams.

Article 17

The official calendar of the country is based on the *hijra* (migration of the Prophet of Islam from Mecca to Medina) and the *hijri* solar and the *hijri* lunar both calendars are equally valid. However, the state administration shall use the *hijri* solar calendar. The weekly official day of rest is Friday.

Article 18

The official flag of Iran is green, white and crimson colours with the particular insignia of the Islamic Republic and the inscription "*Allah-o-Akbar*" (God is Great).

Chapter III

The Rights of the People

Article 19

The people of Iran, of whatever nationality or tribe may be, enjoy equal rights and their colour, ethnic origin, language and the like not be the basis of discrimination.

Article 20

All members of the nations, whether men or women, have equal protection of the law and enjoy all human, political, economic, social and cultural rights in conformity with the Islamic norms.

Article 21

The state is duty-bound to guarantee the rights of women in all spheres in conformity with the Islamic norms and carry out the following:

1. Creation of an environment conducive to the growth of the personality of the woman and restoration of her material and intellectual rights.

2. Support to mothers, particularly during pregnancy and child rearing as well as support to children without a guardian.

3. Creation of competent courts for the protection of the family system and preservation of the family.

(a) Launching of special insurance scheme for the widows, aged and destitute women.

(b) Granting of guardianship over children to worthy mothers for their upkeep in case there is no legal guardian.

Article 22

The status, life, property, rights dwelling-place and the jobs of the individuals are immune from transgression except in matters provided for by the law.

Article 23

Interrogation about a person's beliefs is forbidden and nobody shall be subjected to interference or prosecution merely on the ground of holding a particular belief.

Article 24

Publications and press are free in the expression of their views except when they are detrimental to the fundamentals of Islam or rights of the people. Suspension of this freedom shall be provided for under the law.

Article 25

Inspections and non-delivery of letters, tapping and divulging telephonic conversations, divulgence of telegraphic and telex communications, censorship and failure to transmit or deliver messages, eavesdropping and all kinds of espionage are prohibited except as provided for under the law.

Article 26

Formation of parties, groups, political and professional associations or Islamic associations or associations of recognized religious minorities is permitted provided they do not contravene the national independence, national unity, Islamic norms or the foundations of the Islamic Republic. Nobody can be prevented from joining them nor compelled to join any of them.

Article 27

Assemblies and rallies without bearing of arms are permitted provided they are not detrimental to the fundamentals of Islam.

Article 28

Everybody has the right to take a job of his choice that is not against Islam or public interests or the rights of others.

Article 29

Enjoyment of social security benefits such as in the case of retirement, unemployment, old age, disability, destitution, being stranded in the way, accidents and calamities, need for healthcare and medical care and medical services in case of insurance, etc., shall be a right of all the people.

The state is enjoined in accordance with the law to ensure the provision of requisite services and financial support to each person in the country out of the national revenues and personal contributions.

Article 30

The state is enjoined to provide free education and training to the whole nation up to the secondary level and free higher education to the extent of national self-sufficiency.

Article 31

Having a dwelling-place in proportion to need is a right of each Iranian person and family. The state is enjoined to accord priority to the most needy particularly the rural folk and workers and thus prepare the ground for the enforcement of the provisions of this article.

Article 32

Nobody can be arrested except under the procedure laid down by the law. In case of arrest the charge and reasons for arrest must be communicated without delay in writing to the accused and within a period of 24 hours the charge sheet must be filed before competent judicial authorities for speedy trial of the case. Violators of this article shall be punishable under the law.

Article 33

Nobody can be expelled from the place of his residence or prohibited from residing in a place of his liking or compelled to reside in a place except in cases provided for by the law.

Article 34

Right to judicial remedies is a recognised right of every person and everybody is entitled to approach the competent courts to seek justice. All persons have a right of access to such courts and nobody can be prevented from approaching a court which is competent to deal with the case under the law.

Article 35

In all courts of law both parties to a case have the right to choose their counsel and if they have no means to engage a lawyer they should be provided with the service of a lawyer.

Article 36

The awarding of punishments and their execution is possible only through a competent court of law and in accordance with the law.

Article 37

Everybody is presumed innocent and cannot be considered an offender unless his offence is of proved before a competent court of law.

Article 38

All forms of torture to extract a confession or obtain information is forbidden. Compulsion of any person to give evidence, or make confession or take an oath is unlawful. Any such evidence or confession or oath shall have no value and no validity.

The violator of this Article shall be punishable.

Article 39

Violation of the honour and dignity of a person who has been arrested or detained or imprisoned or exiled in any manner whatever is forbidden and punishable.

Article 40

Nobody can exercise his own right as a means to inflict harm to others or transgress the public interest.

Article 41

Citizenship of Iran is a recognized right of every Iranian. The state cannot terminate the citizenship of any Iranian unless requested by him or unless he acquires the citizenship of another country.

Article 42

Foreign nationals may acquire Iranian citizenship within the limits of the law and citizenship of such persons may be terminated in case they acquire the citizenship of another country or themselves make a request for such termination.

Chapter IV

Economic and Financial Affairs

Article 43

With a view a guaranteeing the economic independence of the society and elimination of poverty and providing for human needs in the course or growth with human freedom the economy of the Islamic Republic shall be governed by the following principles:

1. Provision for the basic needs: housing, food, clothing, healthcare, medical treatment, education and training and necessary facilities for all to form a family.

2. Provision of conditions and opportunities of work for all with a view to achieving full employment and putting means of work in the hands of those who are able to work out do not have the means, by way of cooperatives, interest-free loans or any other legitimate way so that wealth is not concentrated in and does not circulate among a few individuals and groups nor the state is turned

into a totalitarian big employer. This action should take place with due regard to the needs of general economic planning in the country in each of the stages of economic growth.

3. The economic development of the country should be planned in such a way that the form, substance and working hours are such that allow each person enough leisure and energy after his economic pursuits to engage in his spiritual, political and social development and active participation in the leadership of the country and enhancement of his expertise and creativity.

4. Regard for the freedom to choose jobs, non-compulsion of persons to undertake fixed work and protection of the people against exploitation.

5. Prohibition of inflicting harm on others, of monopolies, hoarding, usury and other void and illicit dealings.

6. Forbidding extravagance and wastage of resources in all affairs connected with the economy and in general consumption, investment, production, distribution and services.

7. Utilization of science and technology and of experts for the sake of economic development and advancement of the country.

8. Safeguarding against economic domination of the national economy of the country.

9. Emphasis on increasing productivity of agriculture, animal husbandry and industry to

meet the needs of the public and to attain national self-reliance and to get rid of dependence.

Article 44

The economic system of the Islamic Republic of Iran is composed of state, cooperative and private sectors and is organized according to systematic and sound planning.

The state sector includes all the heavy industries, capital industries, foreign trade, big mines, banking, insurance, energy, dams and barrages, water supply networks, radio and television, posts and telegraph, telephone, civil aviation, shipping, roads and railways and the like. All of them are under public ownership and managed by the state.

The cooperative sector includes all the companies and cooperative societies of production and distribution in urban and rural areas which are formed in accordance with Islamic rules.

The private sector includes that part of activities in agriculture, animal husbandry, industry and trade and services that is complementary to the economic activities of the public and cooperative sectors.

Ownership in these three sectors to the extent that it conforms with the other Articles of this Chapter and is not beyond Islamic laws and contributes to economic growth and development of the country and does not bring harm to the society enjoys the support of the law of the Islamic Republic.

Detailed rules, jurisdictions and conditions of work of three sectors are laid down by the law.

Article 45

Public lands and natural resources or the kind of wasteland or reclaimed lands, mines, rivers, lakes, rivulets and the rest of public water resources, mountains, passes, jungles, swamps, natural groves, unenclosed pastures, property without an heir, properties whose ownership is unknown, and public properties recovered from the usurpers are at the disposal of the Islamic government so that it acts in relation to them in accordance with the public interest. The details and manner of utilization of each one of them are laid down by the law.

Article 46

Everybody is the owner of the product of his acquisition and legitimate work. And nobody can on the strength of his ownership of his own acquisition and work deprive others of the opportunity of acquisition and work.

Article 47

Private property acquired by legitimate means is respectable. The rules in this regard are laid down by the law.

Article 48

In the exploitation of the natural resources and utilization of national revenues at the level of the provinces and regions it is incumbent that there is no discriminating so that each region has access to its necessary capital and opportunities to meet its needs and provide for its growth.

Article 49

The state is duty-bound to confiscate and return to the rightful owners and in case owners are unknown to the public exchequer all wealth derived from usury, usurpation, bribes, cheating, thefts, gambling, misuse of the *waqf* properties, misuse of public contracts and deals, sales of waste-lands and public resources, establishment of places of corruption and all other illegitimate means. Orders in this regard should be implemented after this regard after proper investigations conducted by the state and on the basis of legal proofs.

Article 50

In the Islamic Republic the protection of the biosphere in which the present generation and the future generations shall lead their collective existence is regarded as a public duty. From this view any activities economic or other that pollute the biosphere or inflict irreparable damage to it are forbidden.

Article 51

No taxation can be imposed except under the authority of law. Any amnesty or rebate or tax reductions shall be regulated by the law.

Article 52

The annual budget of the country is prepared by the government in accordance with the procedure laid down under the law and is submitted for the examination and approval of the Islamic consultative Assembly. No alteration in the appropriations can be made except under procedure laid down by the law.

Article 53

All revenue receipts of the state are credited to the general account of the Treasury and no money can be withdrawn except in accordance with appropriations made under the law.

ssssssArticle 54

The National Court of Accounts (*Diwan-i-Mohasebat-i-Kishwar)* shall be directly under the supervision of the Islamic Consultative Assembly. Its organisation and functioning in Tehran and the provincial capitals shall be determined by the law.

Article 55

The Court of Accounts shall, in the manner prescribed by law, scrutinize and audit all accounts of ministries, government agencies, government companies and all other organizations that in one way or another derive benefits from the national budget so that no expenditure is made in excess of the money appropriated and no expenditure is made except for the purpose specified. The Court of Accounts shall collect all the accounts, and related documents in accordance with the law of consolidation of accounts and discharging of the budget and shall report the same each year to the Islamic Consultative Assembly with its own views. This report should be made accessible to the public.

Chapter V

National Sovereignty and Powers Derived from It

Article 56

The absolute sovereignty over the world and the mankind belongs to God and He himself has made man sovereign over his own social destiny. Nobody can deprive man of this divine right or deploy it in the service of the interests of particular individuals and groups. The nation shall exercise this right in ways as specified under the subsequent articles.

Article 57 (amended in 1989)

The governing authorities in the Islamic Republic of Iran are: the Legislature, the Executive and the Judiciary which shall operate under the superintendence of the Supreme Governor and the Leader of the Community in accordance with the subsequent articles of this Constitution.

Article 58

The exercise of the legislative power is vested in the Islamic Consultative Assembly which is composed of representatives elected ay the people and all legislation approved by it after passing the stages as laid down hereafter shall be transmitted to the executive and judicial branches for execution.

Article 59

The legislative power may in respect of some most crucial economic, political, social and cultural issues be exercised by means of a referendum or direct reference to the people to elicit their opinion. The demand for referring a matter to the people for their opinion must be approved by a two-thirds majority of the total number of the representatives of the Majlis.

Article 60 (amended in 1989)

The executive power shall, except in matters directly assigned to the Supreme reader under this Constitution, be exercised by the President of Republic and the Ministers.

Article 61

The judicial power shall be exercised by the courts of justice constituted in accordance with Islamic standards and shall deal with the settlements of claims, protection of people's right, dispensation of justice and enforcement of the divine (*Hudood*).

Chapter VI: *The Legislative Power*

Section 1: The Islamic Consultative Assembly

Article 62

The Islamic Consultative Assembly is constituted of representatives elected directly by the people by secret ballot. Conditions of eligibility of voters and candidates and electoral procedures shall be laid down by the law.

Article 63

The tem of Islamic consultative Assembly is fixed at four years. The election for each term shall be conducted before the expiry of previous term so that at no time the country is left without a Majlis.

Article 64 (amended in 1989)

The strength of the Islamic Consultative Assembly is fixed at 270 members. But after every ten years since the date of holding of the referendum in 1969 taking into account demographic, political, geographical and similar factors a maximum of 20 more members may be added.

The Zoroastrians and the Jews shall elect one representative each, and the Assyrian and Chaldean Christians together one representative and the Armenian Christians of the north and south shall elect one representative each.

The boundaries of electoral constituencies and the numbers of the representatives shall be fixed by the law.

Article 65

After the conclusions of elections the meetings of the Islamic Consultative Assembly have legality in the presence of two-thirds of the total number of the representatives and the approval of proposals and bills in accordance with the internal code of procedure of the Majlis takes place in the same way excejpt in matters for which the Constitution has fixed a special quorum. For the approval of the code of internal procedure the presence of two-third members is compulsory.

Article 66

The manner of the election of the speaker and the presidium and the number of commissions and their term of office and matters connected with debates and internal administration of the Majlis are regulated by the code of internal procedure of the Majlis.

Article 67

The representatives shall in the first sitting of the Majlis take the following oath and sign the oath-deed:

> "In the name of God, the compassionate, the merciful, I in face of the holy Quran swear by God Almighty and on the strength of my human dignity undertake to be the protector of the land of Islam and the guardian of the fruits of the Islamic revolution of the Iranian nation and of the foundations of the Islamic Republic. The trust that the nation has reposed in us I shall preserve as a faithful trustee and in the fulfillment of my function of representation shall maintain my trustworthiness and piety and shall always be bound by the independence and excellence of the country and protection of the rights of the people and service to the people. I shall defend the Fundamental Law

and in my speeches, writings and expressions of opinion shall always keep in view the freedom of people and preservation of their interests."

The representatives of the religious minorities will swear by their own holy book.

Representative who miss the first meeting of the Majlis should perform the ceremony of oath-taking in the first meeting attended by them.

Article 68

In times of war or military occupation of the country, on the proposal of the President of the Republic and after ratification by three-fourth of the total number of the representatives and concurrence of the Guardian Council, elections in the occupied areas or the whole of the country may be suspended for a fixed term and in the event of non-election of a new majlis the previous Majlis shall continue to perform its functions.

Article 69 (amended in 1989)

The deliberations of the Islamic Consultative Assembly shall be open and their complete report shall be broadcast on radio and published in the official gazette for the information of the people. During emergencies, if required by national security and on the demand of the President of the Republic or any one of the ministers or tan representatives, the session of the Majlis may be held in camera. The resolutions of a secret session are valid only if voted upon by three-fourth of the total number of the representatives in the presence of the Guardian Council. After the termination of the emergency the deliberations and the decisions of the secret sessions must be published for the information of the general public.

Article 70 (amended in 1980)

The President of the Republic, his assistants, and the ministers are entitled to attend the open meetings of the Majlis collectively and individually. They may be accompanied by their advisers. Whenever the representatives deem it necessary they call for the presence of the ministers and the ministers are bound to present themselves, whenever the ministers so demand their views must be heard by the Majlis.

Section 2

Powers and Competence of the Islamic Consultative Assembly

Article 71

The Islamic Consultative Assembly may enact laws on general matters within the limits fixed under the Fundamental Law.

Article 72

The Islamic Consultative Assembly cannot enact laws that are contrary to the official religion of the country or the Fundamental Law. Determination of this matter is the responsibility of the Guardian Council in accordance with Article 96.

Article 73

The explication and interpretation of ordinary laws is within the competence of the Islamic Consultative Assembly. The substance of this Article does not detract from the competence of the judiciary to interpret the laws to determine the rights.

Article 74

All legislative bills after clearance by the cabinet are presented to the Majlis. Similarly, legislative proposals on the initiative of at least 15 representatives my be submitted for the consideration of the Majlis.

Article 75

Legislative bills, proposals and amendments to bills drought by the representatives that result in the diminution of general revenue or increase in general expenditure are acceptable for consideration by the Majlis only if they also make a provision to compensate for the deficit in revenue or increase in the expenditure.

Article 76

The Islamic Consultative Assembly has the power to inquire into and investigate all affairs of the country.

Article 77

All international treaties, protocols, contracts and agreements must be ratified by the Islamic Consultative Assembly.

Article 78

All sorts of alteration in the boundaries of the country is forbidden except minor changes in the interest of the country provided these are not unilateral and not stride at the independence and territorial integrity of the country and are approved by four-fifth of the total number of representatives in the Islamic Consultative Assembly.

Article 79

Promulgation of martial law is forbidden, in the event of a war or any such emergency conditions the state has the right with the concurrence of the Islamic Consultative Assembly to impose restrictions temporarily but that duration may not exceed thirty days and in case the necessity persists the government is bound to seek a fresh authorization from the Majlis.

Article 80

Taking or giving of loans or grants internally and externally on the part of the government requires the approval of the Majlis.

Article 81

Giving of licence to foreigners to form companies and organizations in matters of trade, industry, agriculture and mines and services in the country is absolutely prohibited.

Article 82

Employment of foreign experts by the government is forbidden except whenever necessary by the approval of the Majlis.

Article 83

State buildings and properties that are national heritage may not be transferred, to others except with the approval of the Majlis and that also in the circumstance that such heritage should not be associated with a particular person.

Article 84

Every representative is accountable to the whole nation and has the right to express his opinion on all internal and external affairs.

Article 85

The membership of the Majlis is personal to a representative. It cannot be delegated to anybody else. Similarly the Majlis is not competent to delegate its legislative function to a person or body of persons.

However, in respect of certain indispensable matters the Majlis may authorize, in accordance with Article72, its internal commissions to enact the requisite legislation which shall remain in force on an experimental basis for such duration as is determined by the Majlis. All such acts shall be subject to the final approval of the Majlis.

Likewise, the Islamic Consultative Assembly is empowered to delegate the power of approving the charters of organizations, companies, public bodies and attached institutions, with due regard to Article 72, to the concerned (parliamentary) commission or Authorize tri government to grant a charter on its own. In the latter case the action of the government must not be inconsistent with the norms or ordinances or the official religion of the state or the Fundamental Law. The determination of this matter (of inconsistency) lies with the Guardian Council as provided under Article 96. In addition, such government action should also not be contrary to the public laws and rules. With a view to provide for the scrutiny and declaration of their non-repugnancy to the laws it is required that the President of the Majlis (the Speaker) be informed before these charters are transmitted for enforcement.

Article 86

The representatives of the Majlis in the course of discharging their representational functions are absolutely free to express their views and opinions and cannot be prosecuted or detained because of the opinions expressed or the votes by them while performing their functions as representatives.

Article 87 (amended in 1989)

The President of the Republic shall seek the confidence of the Majlis in his council of ministers whenever he constitutes it and before initiating any major programme. During his term he may also seek the confidence of the Majlis in his council of ministers in respect of measures of major public importance or controversial measures.

Article 88 (amended in 1989)

If a minimum of one fourth members of the Majlis direct a question on any matter to the President or Republic or if any one representative directs a question to a minister regarding his functioning the President of the Republic or the minister concerned is bound to present himself to answer to the question raised. The answer may not be delayed beyond one month in the case of the President of the Republic and ten days in case of a minister except for a reason communicated to the Majlis.

Article 89 (amended in 1989)

The representatives of the Islamic Consultative Assembly may in matters deemed by them as important, may call the council of ministers or individual ministers to explain themselves (before the Majlis). Such motions for calling for explanations must be presented to the Majlis with the signatures of at least tan representatives.

The council of ministers or the individual minister called to explain themselves/himself must present themselves/himself before the Majlis within ten days of the tabling of such motions in the Majlis to reply to the motion and seek a vote of confidence. In case of failure of the council of ministers or a minister to tender an explanation the representatives concerned may give necessary clarifications regarding their motion to the

Majlis. The Majlis them may pass a motion of no-confidence, if it deems it necessary.

If the Majlis does not pass a vote of confidence the council of ministers or the minister concerned stands dismissed from office. In both cases the concerned ministers may not be included in the ministry that may be reconstituted thereafter.

In case a minimum of one third of the representatives in the Majlis call the President of the Republic to explain himself in respect of the discharge of his general executive functions and the conduct of state administration the President of the Republic must, within a month of tabling of such a motion, present himself to the Majlis and submit adequate clarifications in respect of matters raised.

In case after hearing the statements of the representatives for and against the motion and they reply of the President of the Republic to it a two-third majority of the total members of the Majlis vote on the incompetence of the President of the Republic a recommendation for his removal from office shall be transmitted to the Supreme Leader in terms of Clause 10 of Article 110.

Article 90

If any person has a complaint regarding the style of functioning of the Majlis or the executive branch or the judicial branch he may present his complaint to the Majlis in writing. It is the duty of the Majlis to look into the complaint and give a satisfactory answer. If the complaint relates to some matter connected with the executive or the judicial branch the Majlis seeks their action and satisfactory reply and transmits the result in fair time. In matters which are connected with the general public it is circulated for general information.

Article 91 (amended in 1989)

To safeguard against the inconsistency of Majlis enactments with the Islamic norms or with the Fundamental law a council designated as the Guardian shall be constituted in the following manner.

Six members from among the just (religious jurists) who are familiar with the requirements of the time and contemporary problems. The choice of this group lies with the Leader.

Six persons from among lay Muslim lawyers specializing in different branches of law whose names are forwarded by the President of the Judicial branch to the Majlis which formally elects them by its vote.

Article 92

The members of the Guardian Council are elected for first session a terms of six years but in the after expiry of three years half members of each group are retired by means of a toss and new members are selected in their place.

Article 93

The Islamic consultative Assembly without the existence of the Guardian Council has no legal validity except in matter of approval of the credentials of the representatives and election of six lawyer-members of the Guardian Council.

Article 94

All enactments of the Islamic Consultative Assembly must be transmitted to the Guardian Council. The

Guardian Council is bound to examine, within a maximum period of ten days of their receipt, their conformity with the Islamic norms and the Fundamental Law. If it finds them inconsistent with the Islamic norms or the Constitution it may send them back to the Majlis for revision. Otherwise the enactment is fit for enforcement.

Article 95

Whenever the Guardian Council does not find the period of ten days sufficient for consideration and final opinion on a bill it may ask the Majlis to extend the period for another ten days by starting its reasons.

Article 96

Determination of non –repugnancy of the enactments of the Islamic Consultative Assembly to the Islamic norms lies with the Fuqaha (religious jurists) of the Guardian Council and determination of their inconsistency with the Constitution lies with the majority of all the members of the Guardian Council.

Article 97

The members of the Guardian Council may, with a view to expedite a matter attend the meetings of the Majlis when it is discussing a legislative bill or proposal and listen to the debate. However, if an urgent bill or proposal is under consideration the members of the Guardian Council must attend the meeting and express their views.

Article 98

Interpretation of the Constitution is the responsibility of the Guardian Council which is discharged with the approval with the approval of three-fourth of them.

Article 99 (amended in 1989)

The Guardian Council is responsible for supervising the elections to the assembly of Experts for the Leadership, the Presidency of the Republic, the Islamic Consultative Assembly, and the elicitation of the public opinion popular referendums.

Chapter VII

The Consultative Councils

Article 100

For speedy implementation of social, economic, development, health, cultural, educational and all welfarist plans in cooperation with the people with regard to the local requirements, the administration of affairs of each village, rural district, city, county or province shall be carried on under the supervision of *Shura* (consultative council) of the village, district, city, county or province and their members shall be elected by the people of the concerned locality.

The qualifications of the electors and the candidates, the limits of their powers and functions, the manner of their election, supervision over these councils and their hierarchical order that must conform with the principle of national unity and territorial integrity, the system of the Islamic Republic and subordination to the central government are determined by a law.

Article 101

With a view to prevent discrimination and secure cooperation of all in the preparation of developmental and welfare plans for the provinces and supervision over their coordinated implementations, a High Consultative

Council of the Provinces shall be constituted of all the members of all the provincial councils.

The manner of the composition and functions of this council shall be determined by a law.

Article 102

The High Consultative Council of the Provinces shall be empowered to prepare plans and schemes and submit them either directly or through the government to the Islamic Consultative Assembly. These schemes shall be considered by the Assembly.

Article 103

Provincial governors (*ostandars*), county heads (*farmandars*), direct heads (*Bakhshdars*) and all other government officials shall be bound to pay due regard to the decisions of these councils made with their jurisdictions.

Article 104

With a view to ensure Islamic equity in the preparation of plans and coordination in the performance of tasks in the productive, industrial and agricultural units consultative committees (*shura*) composed of the representatives of workers, farmers and other functionaries and managers and likewise in the educational, administrative and service units consultative committees composed of representatives of the members of these units shall be created.

Article 105

The decisions of these shuras should not be contrary to Islamic norms and the laws of the country.

Article 106

The dissolution of these shuras except in case of their deviation from their official functions is not possible. The authority entitles to determine the occurrence of deviation, the manner of their dissolution and their reconstitution shall be determined by the law.

Chapter VIII

The Leader

Article 107 (amended in 1989)

After the passing away of the Exalted Source of Emulation, the Great Leader of the Islamic Revolution and the founder of the Islamic Republic of Iran, the Grand Symbol of God Imam Khomeini who was recognized and accepted as the source of emulation and the leader of the community by an overwhelming majority of the people, the election of Leader (Rahbar) is the responsibility of an Assembly of Experts (*Majlise-i-Khobregan*) elected directly by the people.

The Experts shall discuss and deliberate among themselves over the names of all religious jurists (*Fuqaha*) who fulfil the necessary conditions of leadership as laid down under Articles 5 and 109. If they find one of them as most learned (*A'lam*) in the field of Islamic ordinances and jurisprudence, or most learned in social and political affairs, or commanding mass popularity, or being preeminent in any one of the qualities as laid down under Article 109 they may select him as the Leader. Otherwise, they may designate and introduce any one of them as the Leader. The Leader so elected shall be entrusted with *Vilayat-i-Amr* (governance of the affairs of the community) and all responsibilities emanating from this.

This Leader shall be equal with all other members of the state before the law.

Article 108 (amended in 1989)

The law concerning the number and qualifications of the experts, the manner of their election and the rules of internal procedure of their meetings in the maiden session shall be prepared by the religious jurists of the Guardian Council, adopted by their majority and finally approved by the Leader of the Revolution. Thereafter, the amendments and revision of the law and adoption of rules concerning the functioning of the experts shall lie within the competence of the Experts themselves.

Article 109 (amended in 1989)

The Qualification and qualities of the Leader shall be as follows:

1. Necessary academic competence to declare legal opinion (*fatwa*) under different branches of Islamic jurisprudence.

2. Qualification of justice and piety as required for the leadership of the Islamic community.

3. Sound political and social knowledge, statesmanship, courage, managerial skills and adequate competence for leadership.

In case multiple persons are found possessing these qualities one who possesses strongest knowledge in jurisprudence and politics shall have precedence.

Article 110 (amended in 1989)
The functions and powers of the Leader are:

1. Determination of the general policies of the system of the Islamic Republic in consultation with the Board for the Identification of the Expediency of the System.

2. Superintendence over the implementation of the general policies of the system.

3. Issuing proclamations for holding of referendums.

4. Supreme Command of the armed forces.

5. Declaration of war, conclusion of peace and mobilization of armed forces.

6. Appointment, dismissal and acceptance of resignations of the following:

(a) the *fuqaha* (religious jurists) of the Guardian Council.

(b) the head of the judicial branch.

(c) the head of the Radio and Television Organization of the Islamic Republic or Iran.

(d) the chief of the general staff.

(e) the commanding officer of the Islamic Revolutionary Guards.

(f) the commanding officers of the army and the police force.

7. Adjustment of the differences among the three branches of government and organization of their interrelationships.

8. Elimination, through the medium of the board for the identification of Expediency of the System, of the difficulties of the system which cannot be dealt with in an ordinary way.

9. Signing the order for the installation of the President of the Republic after his election by the people. The eligibility of the candidates for the office of the President of the Republic must be confirmed by the Guardian Council and for the first term also by the Leader.

10. Dismissal of the President of the Republic in the interest of the state after the Supreme Court has passed an order regarding dereliction of duty on his part, or the Majlis has passed a vote regarding his incompetence, under Article 89.

11. Granting of pardons and reprieves to convicts on the advice of the President of the Judicial, Branch.

The Leader is empowered to delegate some of his powers and functions to other functionaries.

Article 112 (amended in 1989)

A Board for the Identification of the Expediency of the System (*Majma-i-Tashkhis-i-Maslehat-i-Nizam*) shall be constituted by an order of the Leader with a view to identifying the interest of the system in case a bill passed by the Islamic Consultative Assembly is declared inconsistent with the Islamic norms or the fundamental Law but the Islamic Consultative Assembly taking into account the interest of the system does not agree with the ruling of the Guardian Council the Expediency Board resolves such disputes by a vote of its; to deliberate over matters referred to the Board by the Leader; and to perform ail functions as laid down under this law.

The permanent and variable members of the Board shall be appointed by an order of the Leader.

Rules government the functioning of the Board shall be adopted by themselves with the approval of the Leader.

Chapter IX: *The Executive Power*

Section 1: The President of the Republic and Ministers

Article 113 (amended in 1989)

Next to the office of the Leader, the President of Republic is the highest office-bearer of the state. He shall be responsible for the enforcement of the fundamental law and shall preside over the executive branch except in matters directly assigned to the Leader.

Article 114

The President or the Republic is elected by the direct vote of the people for a term of four years. He can be reelected only for another consecutive term.

Article 115

The President of the Republic must be elected from religious and political figures possessing the following qualifications:

He must be of the Iranian origin, an Iranian citizen, be an administrator and statesman, having good antecedents, be trustworthy, pious, believer and committed to the foundation of the Islamic Republic and the official religion of Iran.

Article 116

The Candidates for the election of the President of the Republic should declare their intention to contest well before the start of the electoral process. The manner of the conduct of presidential election shall be determined by a law.

Article 117

The President of the Republic shall be elected by the vote of an absolute majority of the electorate. But if in the first ballot no candidate secures the votes of an absolute majority a second ballot will be cast to choose between two candidates who secured the largest number of votes in the first ballot. If, however, some candidates securing the largest number of votes in the first round withdraw from the contest then the remaining two candidates securing the largest number of votes in the first round shall contest in the second round.

Article 118

The responsibility for supervision over the election of the President of the Republic lie with the Guardian Council in accordance with Article 99. But before the constitution of the maiden Guardian Council shall be that of a supervisory body established under the law.

Article 119

The election of a new President of the Republic must be held at least one month before the expiry of the term of the incumbent president. During the interregnum between the election of the new president and the end of the term of the previous president the previous president shall continue to perform the functions of the president.

Article 120

Whenever within ten days before the polling one of the candidates whose eligibility was confirmed according to the Constitution dies the polling is postponed by two weeks. If during the interregnum between the first round and the second round one of two candidates who got most numerous votes in the first round dies polling shall be postponed for two weeks.

Article 121 (amended in 1989)

The President of the Republic in a session of the Islamic Consultative Council attended by the President of Judicial Branch and the Guardian Council shall take the following oath and sign the oath-deed:

> "In the name of God, the compassionate, the merciful. I, as the President of the Republic, do swear to God before the Holy Quran and before the Iranian nation that I shall remain the guardian of the Official religion and of the system of the Islamic Republic and the Constitution of the country and shall exercise all my abilities in the way of discharging the responsibilities that I have assumed; that I shall devote myself to the service of the people and progress of the country, propagation of religion and morality; that I shall uphold right and promote justice, desist from self seeking and support the dignity of persons arid their rights as granted by the Constitution; that I shall leave no effort unspared in the defence of the country's

frontiers and political, economic and cultural independence and with God's help and obedience to the Prophet and the Holy Imams I shall guard as a pious and self-sacrificing trustee the power that the nation has put in my hands as a sacred trust and that I shall transfer the same to one who is elected by the nation after me".

Article 122 (amended in 1989)

Within the limits of his powers and functions as assigned to him under this Constitution or the ordinary laws the President of the Republic is responsible before the nation, the Leader and the Islamic Consultative Assembly.

Article 123

The President of the Republic is bound to sign the acts of the Majlis or the results of the referendums when they are presented to him after passing the legal stages, and to transmit the same to the functionaries concerned for execution.

Article 124 (amended in 1989)

The President of the Republic is entitles to appoint assistants to assist him in the performance of his legal functions. The First Assistant to the President shall with his consent look after the cabinet affairs and coordinate between and among the offices of the Presidential Assistants.

Article 125

The President of the Republic or his legal representative is empowered to sign treaties, protocols, agreements and contracts of Iran with all other countries and conventions relating to international organizations subject to the ratification of the Islamic Consultative Assembly.

Article 126 (amended in 1989)

The President of the Republic is directly responsible for planning and budgeting and the administration and personnel of the government. He may delegate this function to some other functionary.

Article 127 (amended in 1989)

In case of need the President of the Republic is empowered to appoint a representative or special representative to deal with a specific matte with specific authority, with the approval of the cabinet. Decisions taken by such a representative or representatives in respect of such delegated matter shall have the same status as the decisions of the President the Republic or the cabinet.

Article 128 (amended in 1989)

Iran's ambassador shall be appointed on the proposal of the minister of foreign affairs and the approval of the President of the Republic. The credentials of the ambassadors of Iran shall be signed by the President of the Republic who shall also receive the credentials of the ambassadors of foreign countries.

Article 129

All state honours and decorations shall be awarded by the President of the Republic.

Article 130 (amended in 1989)

The President of the Republic present his resignation to the Leader and shall continue to discharge the duties of his office until his successor is appointed.

Article 131 (amended in 1989)

In the event of death, dismissal, resignation, absence or illness of the President for more than two months or in case the term of the President of the Republic has expired and because of any constraints the new President has not been elected yet an in similar circumstances, the first assistant of the President with the approval of the Leader shall assume the powers and functions of the President of the Republic. A council composed of the Speaker of the Majlis, the President of the Judicial Branch and the First assistant to the President of the Republic shall make fresh arrangements for the election of a new President within a maximum period of 50 days. In the event of the death of the First Assistant or in case other factors prevent him from performing his functions, and also in a situation where the outgoing President had no First Assistant the Leader may appoint some other person in his place.

Article 132 (amended in 1989)

So long as the powers and functions of the President of the Republic are exercised by the first Assistant or some other person appointed under Article 131, the ministers can not be called so explain themselves before the Majlis nor the Majlis can pass a vote of no-confidence in them. Also no revision of the Constitution or holding of a referendum can be contemplated during this interregnum.

Article 133 (amended in 1989)

Ministers selected by the President of the Republic then presented to the Majlis for taking a vote of confidence. With the renewal of a Majlis taking a fresh vote of confidence in the ministry is not required. The number of ministries and their jurisdictions shall be laid down under a law.

Article 134 (amended in 1989)

The Council of Ministers is presided over by the President of the Republic who oversees the work of the ministers. He takes necessary measures to coordinates the functioning of the ministries and of the cabinet and with the cooperation of the ministers lays down the policy and programme of the government and executes the laws.

In case of differences of opinion and/or overlapping of functions of government agencies involving no interpretation or amendment of the law the decision of the Cabinet shall be enforced compulsorily.

The President of the Republic is responsible before the Majlis for all decisions taken by his cabinet.

Article 135 (amended in 1989)

The ministers continue in office till such time as they have not been dismissed or until in consequence of a motion calling on them to explain themselves, or on a request for a vote of confidence the Majlis has not passed a vote of confidence.

Article 136 (amended in 1989)

The President of the Republic may dismiss the ministers. In this case he may seek a vote of confidence from the Majlis for the new minister or ministers. In case one half of the cabinet is changed after taking a vote of confidence, the President of the Republic shall again seek a vote of confidence from the Majlis.

Article 137 (amended in 1989)

Each minister is responsible before the President of the Republic and the Majlis for the functioning of his ministry. For the collective decisions of the cabinet all ministers are collectively responsible for all policy and action of the government.

Article 138 (amended in 1989)

In addition to matters on which the cabinet or a minister is empowered to frame rules to implement the laws the cabinet is also empowered to issue decrees, and frame rules and regulations to perform its executive duties, to implement the laws and to organize administrative agencies. Each minister is also empowered within his jurisdiction and the resolutions of the cabinet to frame rules and regulations, but the substance of these should not be contrary to the letter and spirit of the laws.

Article 139

Any compounding of claims relating to public and government property or their referral to arbitration is subject to the approval of the cabinet and the Majlis must be informed of such cases. In cases where one party to the litigation is a foreigner or in important domestic cases the approval of the Majlis is compulsory. Such important cases are specified in a law.

Article 140 (amended in 1989)

Charges against the President of the Republic, his assistants and ministers in respect or ordinary offences are heard, after a notice issued by the Majlis in this regard, by the ordinary courts of law.

Article 141 (amended in 1989)

The President of the Republic, ministers and civil servants are not entitled to hold more than one official job. Holding of any other job in enterprises whose capital is wholly or partially owned by the government or a public organization, or taking a seat in parliament, or engaging in legal practice before a court of law or engaging in legal consultancy or holding of executive chairmanship or directorship on the boards of directors of private companies, except in cooperative societies within the deportments or agencies concerned, is prohibited. Teaching posts in universities and research institutes are exempt from this prohibition.

Article 142 (amended in 1989)

The assets held by the Leader, the President of the Republic, the ministers and their wives and children, before joining their offices and afterwards are subject to the scrutiny by the President of the Judicial Power to ascertain that they were not multiplied illegally.

Section 2: The Army and the Revolutionary Guards

Article 143

The army of the Islamic Republic or Iran is responsible for safeguarding the sovereignty, territorial integrity and the system of the Islamic Republic in the country.

Article 144

The army of the Islamic Republic of Iran should be an Islamic army ideologically committed and popular and should recruit only decent persons to service who believe in the goals of the Islamic Revolution and are ready to make sacrifice in the cause of their realization.

Article 145

No foreigner can be inducted as member of army or police force of the country.

Article 146

The establishment of any military base of foreign power in the country is prohibited even if it is intended for peaceful purposes.

Article 147

The government should, in the peacetime utilize the members of the array and their equipments in the field of and relief, education, production and the construction struggle in complete conformity with the Islamic norms and to the extent that it does not affect its combat readiness.

Article 148

All forms of personal utilization of the resources and facilities of the army and personal deployment of its members as waiters, personal drivers or the like is prohibited.

Article 149

Promotion and demotion of the army ranks shall be in accordance with the law.

Article 150

The Corps of the Islamic Revolutionary Guards that was formed in the early days of the victory of the Islamic revolution continues to exist to play its role as the guardian of the Islamic Revolution and its achievements. The functions and limits of the responsibility of this force in relation to the function and jurisdiction of other armed forces with an emphasis on brotherly cooperation and coordination among them shall be laid down in a law.

Article 151

In accordance with the Quanic verses: "And prepare for then whatever force you can and the steeds or War to frighten the enemies of Allah and the enemies of yours and others besides them whom you know not, Allah know them," the government is bound to provide a programme and facilities of military training in accordance with Islamic norms so that all persons always possess the armed defensive capacity but holding of arms requires the permission of government authorities.

Chapter X

Foreign Policy

Article 152

The foreign policy of the Islamic Republic of Iran is based on the negation of all forms of domination and dependence, preservation of complete independence and territorial integrity of the country, defence of the rights of all Muslims, non-alignment in relation to imperialist powers and peaceful relations with non-belligerent states.

Article 153

All forms of contracts that lead to the domination of foreign powers of the natural resource and economy the culture, the armed forces and other affairs of the country are forbidden.

Article 154

The Islamic Republic considers the well-being of the human beings in the whole human society as its ideal and recognizes the right of all people of the world to independence, freedom and rule of law and justice. On this oasis, even though the country is committed, to absolute non-interference in the domestic affairs of other countries, it shall support the just struggles, of the weak and downtrodden against the arrogant mighty in all points of the world.

Article 155

The government of the Islamic Republic may grant political asylum to persons who seek it except those who under the law of Iran are considered as dishonest and subversionists.

Chapter XI: *The Judicial Power*

Article 156

The judiciary is an independent power that supports that individual and social rights and is committed to realization of justice and undertakes the following functions:

1. To consider and issue judgments in respect of appeals, transgressions, complaints, adjudication of suits, resolution of disputes and taxing of decisions and action in such part of the *Hisbi* (social control) matters as provided for under the law.

2. To restore public rights and promote justice and legal freedoms.

3. To supervise over proper enforcement of the laws.

4. To detect crimes, award punishments, prosecute the offenders and execute the *Hudood* (Islamic penalties) and rules of the codified Islamic criminal law.

5. To take appropriate preventive measures before the occurrence of crimes and to provide for the reform of the criminals.

Article 157 (amended in 1989)

With a view to enable the judicial branch to discharge it functions in judicial, administrative and executive affairs the Leader appoints a just mujtahid (religious jurist) who must be well-versed in judicial affairs and an able administrator and policy-maker, with the designation of the "President of the Judicial Branch" for a term of five years who is the highest-ranking judicial office-bearer of the country.

Article 158 (amended in 1989)

The functions of the President of the Judicial Power are as follows:

1. Creation of the necessary infrastructure in the judicial branch in proportion to its responsibilities as mentioned under Article 156.

2. Preparation of judicial projects in consonance with the Islamic Republic, And

3. Recruitment of just *Qazis* (judges), their appointment and dismissal, their postings and transfers, allocation of work to then, their promotion and other similar matters in accordance with the law.

Article 159

The official authority to deal with public grievances and complaints is the Ministry of Justice. The constitution of the courts and delimitation of their jurisdiction is governed by the law.

Article 160 (amended in 1989)

The Minister of Justice shall be responsible for all matters connected with the relationship of the Judicial branch with the executive and legislative branches. He is appointed from among a panel of names recommended by the President of the Judicial Branch to the President of the republic. The President of the Judicial Branch is empowered to delegate all his financial and administrative powers in the respect of recruitment and deployment of non-judicial staff to the Minister of Justice. In this respect the Minister of Justice shall exercise his powers and functions in the same way as visualized by the law for the highest functionaries in the ministries.

Article 161 (amended in 1989)

A Supreme Court (*Diwan-i-Aliyy-i-Kishwar*) shall be constituted in accordance with rules framed by the President of the Judicial Power to oversee the proper application of laws by the courts, to bring about uniformity of judicial rulings and to perform such other functions as entrusted to the under the law.

Article 162 (amended in 1989)

The President of the Supreme Court and the Prosecutor-General both must be just Mujtahids, well-versed in judicial matters and they will be appointed by the President of the Judicial branch for a term of five years after consultation with the judges of the Supreme Court.

Article 163

The qualities and qualifications of the Qazi (religious judge) in conformity with fight standards shall be laid down by the law.

Article 164

No judge can be removed from his post temporarily or permanently without trial and without proof of an offence or misconduct committed by him which required dismissal from service. Nor can the place of his posting or his post except when be changed without his consent except when a decision in this regard is taken by the President of the Judicial Branch in the public interest and after consultation with the Chief Justice and the Prosecutor-General of the Supreme Court. Periodical transfers of judges take place in accordance with general rules laid down by the law.

Article 165

Trials should be conducted in the open and there should be no restriction on the presence of the public except when in the judgment of the court. The open trial may be against public decency or public order or in private litigation the two parties demand that the trial should not be held in the open.

Article 166

The decrees of the courts should be well reasoned and based on specific legal rules and principles.

Article 167

It is the duty of the judge to strive to find the solution of the cases in the codified laws. If he does not find them then by relying on valid Islamic sources or reliable *fatwas* (juristic opinions) he must compose and deliver his judgment. He cannot avoid the consideration of a case and desist from delivering a judgment merely on the ground that the law is silent or it is deficient or it is cursory or that codified laws are mutually conflicting.

Article 168

Trial of political and press cases is public and takes place in the presence of juries in the courts of law. The manner of selection, qualifications, jurisdiction of the juries and the definition of political offences are provided for by the law in accordance with Islamic norms.

Article 169

The commitment or non-commitment of an act cannot be considered as an offence under an *ex post facto* law.

Article 170

The judges of the courts are duty-bound not to enforce any decrees or rules of the government which are contrary to Islamic laws and regulations or are beyond the jurisdiction of the executive branch. Every person has a right to move the Court of Administrative Justice for their invalidation.

Article 171

Whenever a person suffers material or moral harm as a result or the fault or mistake of a judge as to the interpretation of facts or law or application of law to a particular case the committer of the mistake is liable to pay the damage. Otherwise damages are paid by the state and the reputation of the accused is restored.

Article 172

For trial of offences in connection with the military or police functions of the members of the Army, Gendarmerie, Shahrbani (city police) and the Corps of the Revolutionary Guards military courts are constituted in accordance with the law. But ordinary offences or offences committed within the territorial jurisdiction of a police station are tried by the ordinary courts.

Military prosecutors and military courts from part of the judicial system of the country and are bound by the rules of this system.

Article 173 (amended in 1989)

With a view to deal with complaints, grievances and objections of the people pertaining to public servants or government agencies or government regulations or the restoration of the rights of a complainants, a court designated as the Court of Administrative Justice shall be established under the supervision of the President of the Judicial branch. The jurisdiction and the procedure of the court shall be defined by a law.

Article 174 (amended in 1989)

On the basis of the judiciary's right to supervise the proper conduct of affairs and to ensure enforcement of the laws through the administrative agencies an organisation designated as the State Investigation Organization (*sazman-i-bazrasiyy-i-Kull-i-Kishwar)* shall be established under the supervision of the President of the Judicial branch. The jurisdiction and functions of this organization shall be determined by a law.

Chapter XII: *Sada-wa-Seema*

(The Radio and Television Organization)

Article 175 (amended in 1989)

The Radio and television organization of the Islamic Republic is guaranteed freedom of expression and dissemination of opinions with due regard to the Islamic norms and the interests of the state.

The power of appointment and dismissal of the Head of Sada-wa-Seema is vested in the Leader and a council composed of two representative each of the President of the Republic and the President of the Judicial branch shall exercise supervision over this organization.

The policy and administration of the organizations shall be governed by a law.

Article 176 (amended in 1989)

To protect national interests and safeguard the Islamic Revolution and territorial integrity and national sovereignty a High Council of National Security (*Shura-i-Aliyy-i-Amniyyat-i-Milli*) shall be constituted under the headship of the President of the Republic with the following functions.

1. Determination of the defence and security policies of the country within the general policies as approved by the Leader.

2. Coordination between political, intelligence, social, cultural and economic activities in conjunction with the general defence and security measures.

3. Utilization of the material and intellectual resources to meet the internal and external threats.

The Council shall be composed of the following:

- Heads of the three branches of government
- The Chief of the Military Staff
- The Head of Planning and budget Organization

- Two representatives of the Leader
- Ministers of Foreign Affairs, Interior and Intelligence

Each minister in his own functional area and the high rank holder of the Army and the Corps of the National Security Council shall constitute sub-councils like a defence council and an internal security council. The sub-councils shall be headed by the President of the Republic or one of the members nominated by the President.

The jurisdiction and functions of the sub-councils shall be defined by a law and they shall be constituted with the approval of the High Council.

All the decisions of the High Council of National Security shall come into force after the approval of the Leader.

Article 177 (amended in 1989)

Wherever necessary the amendment of the Constitution of the Islamic Republic shall follow the following procedure:

The Leader after consultation with the Expediency Council in an order addressed to the President of the Republic may direct that requisite amendments or complements be referred to a Constitutional Revision Council (*Shura-i-Baznigariyy-i-Qanun-i-Asaasi*) to be constituted in the following manner:

1. All members of the Guardian Council

2. The heads of the three branches of government

3. The permanent members of the Expediency Board

4. Five members of the Assembly of Experts for leadership

5. Ten persons nominated by the Leader

6. Three members of the Council of Ministers

7. Three members of the judiciary

8. Ten members of the Islamic Consultative Assembly

9. Three academics.

The manner of the work, selection of members and their qualifications shall be laid down in a law.

The amendments or additions cleared by the Revision Council after signatures and approval by the Leader shall be referred to the people in a referendum who must approve them by an absolute majority.

It is not necessary to follow the procedure laid down under Article 59 in relation to a constitutional revision.

The principles governing the Islamic character of system, the subordination of all laws and rules to the Islamic norms, the articles of belief and goals of the Islamic Republic, the republican character of the state, the principle of *Vilayat* and leadership of the community, the principle of governance according to the public opinion, and the official religion are not subject to amendment [i.e. are immutable].

Appendix B

The Last Testament of Imam Khomeini*

In the Name of God, the Merciful, the Compassionate

The Prophet of God (Hazrat Muhammad), peace be on him, said:

> "I am leaving unto you the *thaqlain* [two trusts], the Book of God [Quran] and my family. They will not part company until they are returned [to me] at the *Kausar* [the pool of abundance in the paradise"].

I consider it proper to discuss the significance of the "two trusts". It is beyond my capacity and bearing to dwell upon the transcendental, spiritual and mystical dimensions of these two entities; not of what has happened to the mankind for forsaking them; nor of what has to them at the hands of the enemies of God and tyrants as this cannot be accounted by me here for lack of knowledge and opportunity. But I deem it proper to make a very short and passing reference to what has happened to the two trusts.

---

* *Translated from Persian– This testament was written in 1982 but was made public after his death in 1988 in accordance with the instruction of Imam Khomeini.*

Perhaps the utterance: "They shall not part company until they are returned to the pool" is related with the fact that after the sacred existence of the Prophet of God (peace be on him) whatever has happened to one of them has equalty happened to the other and the forsaking of one is tantamount to the forsaking of the other until the time they are united with the Prophet at the pool.

Whether the pool symbolizes the convergence-point of the many in one or submergence of the drops into the river is beyond human comprehension. It may be pointed out merely that the atrocities committed against the two, against the Islamic community and against the mankind are indescribable.

This point is essential as the tradition of the two trusts (*thaqlain*) is common to all sets of the Muslims. The books of the Sunnites, particularly the *Sihah-i-Sitta* [the six collections of the authentic sayings of the Prophet] and others have recorded it though with varying words and overlapping content. This tradition is, therefore, a categorical proof for the whole of the mankind, especially for the Muslims belonging to the different schools.

Now let us see what has happened to the Book of God, that bequest of God, and to the descendants of the Prophet.

The unfortunate developments started unfolding after the martyrdom of Hazrat Ali. The despots and the tyrants made the Quran a tool of their anti-Quranic rule. The actual interpreters of the Quran who had learnt the Quran from the Prophet himself and had still the echo of "I am leaving unto you the two trusts" ringing in their ears, were isolated, the teachings of the Quran, a law for the material and spiritual life of the mankind till its return to the pool, were neutralized, and rule of divine justice enjoined by it nullified and autocratic rule instituted in derogation of the holy book and traditions of the Prophet in such a way that the pen shies from recording them. And what came out of this foundation added more to wrongdoing and deviation so much so that Quran revealed by the God for the guidance of the mankind, ushering an order based on justice and equity and entrusting the governance to vicegerents of God the infallible Imams who would in turn assign it to whosoever was capable to serve the mankind, was excluded from the social sphere as if it had no role in human guidance. Eventually in the hands of the wicked regimes and ignorant preachers (*akhunds)* worse than the tyrants Quran became a tool for justifying corrupt and tyrant regimes and defending the oppressors and the enemies of God. Regrettably, the Quran meant to shape the destinies of the people was left with no role except at the graveyards and funeral ceremonies.

That which was to be a means for uniting the Muslims and the mankind and a book of life became for them a means to create dissensions or excluded from the social sphere altogether. We saw that if anybody spoke about Islamic government was held to have committed a great sin and the political preacher was and still is synonymous with irreligious preacher.

Lastly, the great Satanic powers through the medium of regimes which have forsaken Islamic teachings but still pretend to espouse Islam get the Quran printed in a beautiful face and form and distributed throughout the world only to undermine it and to advance the Satanic objectives of the superpowers. In the Satanic way the Quran is withdrawn from the public sphere. We saw the Quran printed by Reza Khan which numbed the people and some uninformed *akhunds* were all praise for his Islamic deeds. We also see that king Fahd spends people's immense wealth on the printing of Quran and on the preachers of the anti-Quran, baseless and nonsense cult of Wahhabism to draw the unaware people and nations towards the superpowers. He uses dear Islam and the Quran only to undermine Islam and Quran only to undermine Islam and Quran.

We are proud that our dear nation is absolutely committed to Islam and that Islam is proud of presenting a religion that stands not only for the unity of Muslims but of the whole mankind. It must be liberated from mausoleums and graveyards and this greatest charter of liberation of man be allowed to deliver him from all fetters that bind his feet, hands, heart and mind and drive him towards self-destruction, nullity and slavery of the tyrannical powers. We are proud of being followers of a religion founded by the Prophet by the command of God and the Commander of the Faithful Ali Ibne Abi Talib, a person free from all fetters, who was appointed to free the man from all fetters and servitude.

We are proud of the fact that the book *Nihjul Balagha* [a collection of the sermons of Hazrat Ali, according to the Shiite belief] which following the holy Quran is the greatest charter of material and spiritual life, supreme liberator of man, showing him the path of salvation, is from our infallible Imam.

We are proud that the infallible Imams from Ali Ibne Abi Talib to the saviour of the mankind, Mahdi the expected one, who by the divine providence is living and overseeing the affairs of the world.

We are proud that the life-giving prayers (chantings) which infallible Imams. The prayers of the month of *Shaban* [eleventh month of the Islamic lunar calendar], the prayers of Imam Hussain Ibne Ali originally chanted at Mount Arafat, the *Sahifa-i-Sajjadiyya* and the *Sahifa-i-Fatimiyya* given to Fatima Zohra by divine inspiration, all belong to us.

We are proud that Baqar-al-Uloom[the fifth of the twelve Imams], the most outstanding personality in history whose stature cannot be appreciated by anybody except God, his Prophet and the infallible Imams, is of us.

And we are proud of our Jafari school of jurisprudence, an unfathomable river that is his legacy and we are proud of all our infallible Imams and committed to follow them.

We are proud of the fact that in preaching the religion of Islam and putting the teachings of Quran into practice, one of whose commands is establishment of just rule, our infallible Imams suffered imprisonments and exiles and ultimately laid down their lives in their struggle to bring down tyrannical and unjust governments. And today we are proud of desire to realize the objectives of the Quran and the prophetic traditions. In this destiny-making path the different strata of our people sacrificed their life, property and the dear ones in the way of God.

We are proud that the women, young and old, adult and minor, take part in the cultural, economic and military spheres side by side with their menfolk or better than towards Islam and the Quranic objectives. Those who are capable of fighting take part in military training that is one of the important duties for the defence of Islam and the Islamic state. They have courageously and committedly got rid of all lack of knowledge about Islamic and Quranic ordinances that was imposed upon them by the intrigues of enemies or negligence of friends. They have also overcome the nonsensical propaganda launched by the enemies to promote their own interests through ignorant people and some preachers unaware of the true interests of the Muslims. Those who are incapable of fighting render services behind the front so dedicatedly that makes the hearts of the nation throb with joy and the hearts of enemies and the ignorant lot worse than the enemies tremble with rage. We have many times seen the elderly women the like of Zainab crying that they gave their sons in the way of God and Islam and sacrificed everything and were proud of it and knew whatever they achieved was better than the heavenly paradise what to speak of the petty things of this world. Not only our people but all Islamic people know that their enemies are the enemies of God, Quran and Islam. They are savages who do not desist from committing any crime and treachery for attaining their wicked objectives. In the pursuit of domination and their baser interests they do not discriminate between friends and foes. And their overlord is the USA, a terrorist in itself, a government that has set the whole world on fire, whose allies the world Zionists commit such crimes of attain their objectives that the pen is ashamed of writing and the tongue of mentioning them. The stupid idea of greater Israel drives them to commit all sorts of crime against the Palestinians. And the Islamic nation and the downtrodden of the world are proud to know that their enemies are Hussain [of Jordan], the professional criminal, and Hasan [of Morocco] and Honi Mobarak [of Egypt] who in the service of the USA and Israel do not hesitate from committing any treachery to their own nations. And we are proud that our enemy is Saddam Aflaqi recognized by friends and foes alike for his crimes and violations of international law ana human rights. All know that his treachery against the oppressed people of Iraq and the Sheikhdoms of the Gulf is not less than his treachery against the Iranian people. And we are proud that the mass media and propaganda organs directed by the criminal superpowers are accusing us all crime and treachery. What honour is greater and more sublime than this that USA with its tall claims, its military might, its allies, its possession of the wealth of the backward nations and its control of the mass media became helpless and was humiliated in confrontation with the proud Iranian people and the state of Hazrat Baqiyyatullah (the Hidden Imam), may our souls be sacrificed for his recoming. It does not know who to take recourse to and whosoever it turns to gives a negative response. It would not have been possible without the invisible aid of the Almighty who has awakened the nations, particularly the Iranian Islamic nation from the darkness of tyranny to the light of Islam.

Now I advise the noble oppressed nations and the dear Iranian nation that they should adhere to the straight path of God that has no relation with either the atheist east or the infidel oppressive west but is a path ordained by God Almighty. They should not any moment forget to thank Him for this bounty. The unclean hands of the agents of the superpowers both external and internal, the internal being worse than the external, must not shake their pure intention and the iron will and must know that whatever is orchestrated by the global mass media and the Satanic forces of the east or west is a testimony to their own strength and God Almighty will punish them in this world and the world hereafter. He is the donor of all bounties and everything is in his dominion. With all seriousness and humility I beseech the Islamic nations to follow wholeheartedly and diligently the pious Imams and their political, social, economic and military culture. Of all things they should not depart from is classical Islamic jurisprudence (*fiqh*) which explicates the ideas and ideals of the prophetic and Imamite mission. It guarantees the progress and glory of nations. There can be no difference between the primary and secondary ordinances as both belong to the same jurisprudence. They should not lend their ears to the hostile doubt-creators and must know that one deviant step shall be the beginning of the collapse religion and religious ordinances and just rule. One thing they should not miss is the Friday prayer are the greatest blessing of the Almighty to the Islamic Republic. They should not neglect the morning assemblies commemorating the martyrdom of pious Imams, particularly the lord of all martyrs Hazrat Hussain Ibne Ali.

They must know that commemoration of this historic martyrdom (of Imam Hussain) and whatever curses or damnations are raised against their oppressors represents a historic cry of nations against the tyrants throughout history. Remember to damn the house of Umayyads for the atrocities committed by them. May God damn them. Their dynasty became extinct and they were consigned to hell. This damnation is tantamount to a damnation of all the oppressors of the world and keeps alive the cry against tyranny. It is necessary that elegies or prosodies concerning the pious Imams and the tragic episodes and the atrocities committed by the tyrants of all ages and all places be narrated loudly. The present age is an age of oppression of the Islamic world by the Americans and the Soviets and their allies, including the house of Saud, those ill-keepers or the

House of God (Kaaba). May God, his pharisees and his messengers damn them all. They must be damned loudly. Everybody must know that these political ceremonies are conducive to the unity of Muslims, particularly the followers of the twelve Imams, God's blessings and peace be on them.

It must be reminded here that this political divine last testament of mine (*Wasiyyatnameh*) is addressed not only to the noble nation of Iran but is also a piece of advice for all Islamic nations and all oppressed peoples of the world irrespective of nationality and religion.

I humbly pray to God Almighty not to forsake us for moment and not to cease a moment bestowing his blessings upon these children of Islam and the dear combatants.

Ruhullah al-Musavi al-Khomeini

In the Name of God, the Merciful, the Compassionate

The importance of the glorious Islamic Revolution of Iran that is the achievement of millions of zealous people and thousands of martyrs, those eternally alive martyrs who are the focus of the hopes of the millions of Muslims and the downtrodden of the world, is of an order that the pen and tongue are unable to describe. Myself Ruhullah Musavi Khomeini with all my shortcomings am not disappointed of the grace of the Almighty and my wherewithal in my journey to the next world is the same grace of the absolute grace giver.

I am but a humble student and with other brothers-in-faith have high hopes of this Revolution and wish for the perpetuation of its achievements and further fruition. With this last testament I wish to convey certain views, though overlapping, to the present and future generations and pray to forgiving God to infuse me with sincerity of purpose in these submissions.

1. We are aware that this great Revolution which immobilized the world-devourers and the oppressors vis-à-vis great Iran triumphed with invisible divine aid. Without the strong had of God it had no chance. A nation of 30 million was consistently exposed to anti-Islamic and anti-clerical propaganda, particularly over the past 100 years, and to the subversive writings and speeches of the intellectuals through the press and conferences called for propagating [Aryan] nationalism. They were subjected to brothels, casinos, liquor and narcotics. All these were meant to divert the young people, who were expected to work for the progress of their beloved country, to decadence and degeneration. All moves made by the former corrupt Shah and his uncultured father and cabinets handpicked from trumped up parliaments at the behest for foreign embassies made them insensitive to the national cause.

And worse than all was the condition of universities, schools and centres of education and training, which are the custodians of the destinies of a nation. They were packed by either westernized or easternized teachers who in the name of Aryan nationalism were hundred per cent against Islam and the true Islamic national culture. There were some persons devoted and committed to Islam but this tiny minority was in such straits that it could do nothing positive. There were a horde of other problems of which the isolationism of the clergy and the ideological misdirection of many under the influence of official propaganda was one. Without divine support it was not possible for a nation in this condition to rise unitedly in revolt with a single idea and single slogan of *Allah-o-Akbar* (God is Great), offer miraculous sacrifices and defeat the external and internal powers and take their destinies in their own hands.

On this account there can be no doubt that the Islamic Revolution in Iran was distinct from all other revolutions in its origins as well as its motivations and methods. It was no doubt a divine gift and an invisible boon of God bestowed upon the oppressed and dispossessed nation of Iran.

2. Islam and Islamic government are phenomena that ensure the salvation of its followers in this world and in the world hereafter. It is capable of negating all oppression, exploitation, corruption and transgression and leading the men to excellence. It is an ideology which is entirely different from all non-monotheistic ideologies in that it regulates and oversees all personal, social, material, moral cultural and political affairs and does not leave out even minor details in the cultivation of man and society and their guidance towards material and moral progress. It takes due care of obstacles in the way of self-fulfillment of the individual and society and tries to remove them. Here is an Islamic Republic created by the strong hands of a committed nation with divine grace and support and what rules here is Islam and its ordinances. It is obligatory for the noble nation of Islam to strive to realize its essence in all its dimensions and to protect and preserve it. The preservation of Islam is in the forefront of all obligations. All great prophets from Adam (peace be on him) to the last prophet (peace be upon him) have strived and suffered in its cause and no hardship has prevented them from discharging this obligation. Likewise after them the committed companions of the prophet and the holy

Imams have struggled and laid down their lives in its defence. It is incumbent on the Iranian nation and all the Muslims to preserve this divine trust with all their might which has been officially proclaimed in Iran and which has borne fruits in a short time. We must work for its continuation and remove the constraints and obstacles in its way. I hope its light reflects on and illuminates all the Islamic countries and that all states and nations come to an understanding on this on this vital matter and the world devouring powers and criminals of history from the oppressed and suppressed of the world for ever.

Myself towards the end of my life proffer a few suggestions for the preservation and perpetuation of this divine trust and point out to the present and future generations the obstructions and dangers in its way. I pray to the Almighty for the success and support of all.

(A) Indisputably, the secret of the continuity of the Islamic Revolution is the same secret of its triumph and the nations is aware of this secret of victory. The future generations shall read in history that the two cardinal pillars of the Revolution were divinely ordained noble mission of Islamic rule and the convergence of the nation throughout the country on the unity of *Kalimah* (there is no God but one God), and for the realization of this mission.

I advise the present and future generations that if you wish that Islam and divine rule survive in earth and the imperialist and exploiting powers are kept at bay don't forsake this mission which is ordained by God in the holy Quran. The alternative to this mission which is the secret of its triumph and continuity is losing sight of the goal and disintegration and conflict. It is not without purpose that the propaganda apparatuses of the world and their local offshoots are devoting all their energy to spreading rumours and divisive lies and spending billions of dollars for this purpose. It is not without purpose that the enemies of the Islamic Republic make frequent journeys to this region and it is regrettable that among them may be seen the rulers of some Islamic states who don't think beyond their personal interests and blindly submit themselves to Americans. Some pseudo-clergymen are also associated with them. The Muslims of today and tomorrow must be informed about and asked to counteract and neutralize this divisive and subversive propaganda. My advice to the Muslims and particularly to the Iranians of the present day is to take countermeasures against these conspiracies and reinforce their solidarity and unity in all possible ways to disappoint the infidels and the hypocrites.

(B) One of noticeable conspiracies that was hatched during the last century and rehatched during the recent decades particularly since the victory of the Islamic Revolution is the widespread propaganda in different forms to wean away the people, particularly the Iranian people, from Islam, sometimes it is allege crudely and nakedly that Islamic ordinances were devised some 1400 years ago and cannot help in the governance of a modern state or that Islam is a reactionary religion and opposed to every innovation and manifestation of civilization and that in the present age countries should not keep aloof from the world civilization and its manifestations. Other instances of such Satanic and provocative propaganda are that in the name of sanctity of Islam and other religions it is claimed that what all these religions are concerned with is spiritual betterment, keeping distance from the secular authorities, renunciation of worldly pursuits, engagement in worship, prayers and chantings that bring the man near to God keep him way from the world and that government politics and administration are detrimental to the pursuit of this spiritual objective. For, politics is concerned with the betterment of this world, but this view is contrary to the teachings of great prophets. The propaganda of the second variety has influenced some clergymen and religious persons ignorant of Islam so much so that they regard any involvement in government and politics as a sin and bad deed. Perhaps some of them know this a great tragedy that has befallen Islam. The first group is either ignorant of government, politics and law or feigns ignorance for its selfish ends. For enforcement of laws in accordance with norms of equity and justice; elimination of tyranny and despotism; ensuring justice for the individuals and the society; elimination of corruption, obscenity and other forms of deviant behaviour; freedom in accordance with standards of reason, justice, independence, self-reliance; and eradication of colonialism, exploitation and slavery; penalties and sanctions in accordance with justice to forestall corruption and moral degradation; direction of a society according to rationality, equity and justice and hundreds of other such norms do not become obsolete with the passage of time. Such assertions are tantamount to saying that rules of logic and mathematics formulated in the bygone eras should be changed in the modern age. That in the beginning of the creation God may have ordained that justice be established, and tyranny, plunder and murder be checked but not in this atomic age this norm has become obsolete. Similarly, the insinuation that Islam is opposed to innovations or as the or the deposed Muhammad Reza charged that these people want the people to travel in this age by quadruped, is simply stupid. For it by manifestations of civilization is meant inventions, new products and technical advancements that have a role in human progress and advance of civilization neither Islam nor any other monotezeistic religion is or can ever be opposed to them. On the contrary, knowledge and industry have been eulogized in the holy Quran. However, if by freedom is meant, as the professional intellectuals claim, licentiousness such as obscenity or homosexuality and the like all religions and rational men are opposed to it though westernized or easternized liberals may continue to uphold it in emulation of the west or the east. So far as the second group is concerned they propagate a subversive idea of separation of religion from politics. These ignorant people must be told that the holy Quran and the holy Prophet has prescribed more rules for government and politics than for any other sphere. Moreover, many acts of worship in Islam are of political nature negligence of which has brought about all these sufferings. The Prophet of Islam instituted a government similar to other governments of the world but with the unique objective of spreading social justice. The first successors of the Prophet presided over expanded governments, and the government of Ali Ibne Abi Talib having the same objective and being larger and wider was a glaring example in history. Afterwards, governance continued to be carried on in the name of Islam and now there are many exponents of Islamic government by way of following Islam and the Prophet.

Myself in this Testament have made only passing references but hope that writers, sociologists and historians would liberate the Muslims from this misconception. Whatever was said and is being said like the prophets were concerned merely with spiritual salvation and that government and administration was a prohibited for territory for the prophets and men of religion is a devastating mistake which would lead to destruction of the Islamic nations and open the way to the domination of the blood-sucking imperialists. For what is condemned in religion is satanic dictatorial and tyrannical governments which seek only domination and pursue corrupt objectives.

The avoidance of the world which is preached by religions refers to the accumulation of wealth and power despotism and this is the world which makes man forget God Almighty. But the government of justice for the benefit of the downtrodden, uprooting of tyranny and oppression and promulgation of social justice which Prophet Soloman son of David and Prophet Muhammad and his revered successors strived for is one of greatest obligations and its realization is the highest act of worship. That is why clean politics found in these polities is an essential requirement. The awakened and alert people of Iran with an Islamic outlook must rise to aid the nation chopping off the hands of intriguing Satans

(C) And of this category are the intrigues, perhaps more damaging, to spread rumours in the country most of them centring on the point that the Islamic Republic has done nothing for the people; that the helpless people who willingly made sacrifices to overthrow the despotic regime became captives of a worse regime; that the high and mighty became highest and mightiest; the prisons are full of youth who are the hope of the future; that torture inflicted now was worse than under the former regime and more inhuman; that everyday a number of people are being executed in the name of Islam; that better they had not named this Republic as Islamic; that these times were worse than the times of Reza Khan and his son; that people are eking out a miserable existence amids rising prices and high inflation; that the present regime is being run like a communist regime; that property of the people is being expropriated and the nation deprived of its liberties; and so many such things are being circulated in a planned way. The proof of a scheme and an intrigue is that every few days some rumour is on the tongue of the people in every street-corner or roadside and each alley and by lane. The same is repeated in taxies, buses and wherever people assemble. If one becomes a little stale another is made popular. Unfortunately, some clergyman, unaware of these satanic machinations, after meeting one or two such persons involved in these intrigues, become convinced of the veracity of such rumours. The basic malady is that most of those who near and believe in these rumours have no knowledge of the state of the world and other revolutions and post-revolutionary upheaval and unavoidable complications. Therefore they do not have correct information of what is beneficial to Islam and with closed eyes and ignorantly listen to such rumours and thus inadvertently listen to such rumours and thus inadvertently or deliberately become involved in them. I advise you first to study the prevailing conditions in the world and then compare the Islamic Revolution with all other revolutions and become familiar with the conditions of states and nations undergoing revolution and what happened to them after revolution and consider the difficulties facing this oppressed nation through the plundering of Reza Khan and worse than him so Muhammad Reza. That is their legacy for this state. And look at the self-destructive dependencies, the state of ministries, administrative agencies, the economy, the army, the houses of pleasure, narcotic shops, indiscipline in all walks of life, the status of education and training, the status of secondary schools and universities, and the state of cinema houses, the condition of youth and women, the condition of the clergy and the religious class, the plight of freedom-seekers and the oppressed chaste women, and the manner of trial of those sentenced to death or imprisoned and the conditions of persons and the conduct of bureaucracy and consider the assets acquired by the big capitalists, land-devourers, hoarders and profiteers, and consider the courts of justice and revolutionary courts and compare them with the previous condition of the judiciary and the judges, and consider the status of the deputies of the *Majlis-i-Shoora-i-Islami* (The Islamic Consultative Assembly), the members of the government, the provincial governors and the rest of state functionaries appointed during the recent times and compare them with the older times; and consider the working of the government and of the Corps of the Reconstruction Struggle (*Sazmaan-i-Jihad-i-Sazandagi*) in the countryside deprived of basic amenities of life, even the drinking water and dispensaries; and compare them with the whole length of the former regime, especially taking into account the difficulties arising from the Iraq-imposed war (1980-88) and its consequences in the form of millions of displaced persons and destitute families of the martyrs and the sufferers in the zones and millions of Afghan and Iraqi refugees (staying in Iran); and also take into view the economic blockade imposed by the USA and frequent intrigues on its part and the part of its allies both external and internal; and add to all these the lack of the requisite number of religious preachers and Islamic judges (*qazis*) and devastations wrought by the opponents of Islam and the dissidents, even ignorant friends and tens of other problems. I request that unless you become familiar with these complexities don't stand to criticize or create complications or spread obscenity. Have mercy on this poor Islam which after tyrannical rule of the despots throughout centuries and the ignorance of the masses is reborn today and is still an infant surrounded by external and internal enemies. You obstructionists and complications-mongers must sit down to think whether it is not better that instead of destruction lend your hand to the reconstruction programme. Instead of supporting the unjust God-forgetting hypocrites, oppressors, capitalists and hoarders support the oppressed, the tyrannized and the deprived. Instead of giving indirect support to subversive groups and destructive terrorists pay attention to the victims of terrorists, the terrorized men of religion and the tyrannized servants.

I never said nor do I say that today in this republic Islamic is practiced perfectly in all its dimension and that there are not persons who because of their ignorance or their complexes or indiscipline do not act contrary to Islamic principles but I do submit that the legislative, executive and judicial authorities are trying their best to Islamize this country and this thirty million strong nation too aids and supports them. If this complication mongering and disruptive minority hastens to cooperative with us the achievement of this objective becomes easier and speedier. If, God unwilling, these people don't come of their own the awakened millions-strong nation, attentive to the problems, and ready in the sphere of action shall, by the will of God, realize substantially the humanistic-Islamic goals and objectives and the misguided ones and the complication mongers snail not be able to block this roaring flood. I have courage to assert that the millions-strong Iranian nation of this age is in a better situation than the community of Hejaz (Arbia) during the times of the holy Prophet and Iraq, and Kufa during the times of the Commander of the Faithful Hazrat Ali and Hazrat Hussain. In Hejaz during the times of the Prophet the Muslims did not obey him and by making excuses did not go to the war front. God Almighty in Psalm *Tauba* (Repentence) of the Quran rebuked them for their behaviour and warned them of his retribution. They spun so many lies that the Prophet was forced to condemn them from the pulpit. The people of Iraq and Kufa misbehaved so much towards the Commander of the Faithful that the grievances of His Holiness as recorded in history books are well-known. And those Muslims of Iraq and Kufa how did they treat the Lord of Martyrs (Imam Hussain)!And these were the people who did not engage the enemey or fled from the front or sat back in their homes so that historic crime (assassination of Imam Hussain) occurred. However, in today's Iran we see that the Iranian nation with its military and police forces, the Revolutionary Guards, the Baseej (mobilized forces), popular militias, the tribesmen and volunteers, and with the forces at the front and the people behind the front perform acts of self-sacrifice willingly and longinginly and create epics. And we see the honorable people from the whole country extending their valuable assistance. And we see that the dependents of the martyrs and those displaced from the war zone and their relatives meet you and me with heroic faces and seem calm and contended in their speech and countenance. They are all inspired by the love of and belief in God and Islam and in the life eternal. They are not living in the age of the Prophet nor that of the infallible Imams. They are motivated by faith and trust in the invisible. This is the mystery of their success and victory in all its dimensions. Islam must be proud of rearing such children and we are all proud of living in such an age and being in the forefront of such a nation.

And here I tender a piece of advice to such people who with a different motive oppose the Islamic Republic and to the young Boys and girls who have been exploited by the opportunist, self-seeking hypocrites and dissidents. I ask you to sit down and judge impartially and freely the propaganda of those who want the Islamic Republic to go down; their mode of functioning; their attitudes towards the deprived people; the groups and governments that supported them and are still supporting; the individuals and groups that are aligned with them in the country; their behaviour towards their peers and the followers; and look closely at their changing positions on unfolding developments. Read the particulars of those in this Republic who have been assisted by these hypocrites and the disaffected and judge between them and their enemies. Some of the tapes of these martyrs are in our hands and perhaps the tapes of their enemies may be in your hands. See for yourselves which group has served the cause of the deprived and the oppressed in the society.

Brothers! You may not be able to read these pages before my death. May be you read them after my death. At that time I will not be near you to play with your tender hearts to gain power and position. For the reason that you are decent young men I wish you spend your youth in the way of God and Islam and the Islamic Republic. I pray to the merciful Lord that He lead you to the straight path of humanity and with his boundless compassion forgive us and you of our past. You too should pray in privacy to the Almighty for the same; for He is the guide and the compassionate one.

And I offer a piece of advice to the noble Iranian nation and all other nations who suffer at the hands of corrupt regimes and from bondage of great powers. I advise the beloved nation of Iran to recognize like all matters dearest to you the value of that bounty you have attained with your own great struggle and the blood of your brilliant young men. You must defend and preserve it and struggle in its way because it is a great bounty and great trust of God. Don't be afraid of hardship that comes across this straight path as Allah says: "If you help Allah He will help you and make firm your steps." Take part in removing the difficulties of the Islamic Republic with your soul and heart and treat the government and the Majlis (parliament) as of you and safeguard them as precious objects of love and I advise the Majlis and the government and the public servants to recognize the worth of this nation and be active in their service particularly the downtrodden–the deprived and the oppressed sections who are the light of our eyes and beloved of all. The Islamic Republic is their creation and came into being with their sacrifices. Its continuity also depends on their services. Don't forget them. Know yourselves as of the people and the people as of you. Always condemn the tyrannical regimes that were run by uncultured plunderers and mindless liars and still are, albeit in human ways that are befitting an Islamic regime. I advise the other Islamic nations to take the government of the Islamic Republic and the struggling people of Iran as their model and pull down the tyrannical regimes that do not heed the desires of these nations which are the aspirations of the Iranian nation too. For the cause of the misfortunes of Muslims are regimes aligned with either the east or the west. I advise you not to lend your ears to the propaganda organs of the enemies of Islam and the Islamic Republic as all try to exclude Islam so that the interests of the great powers are safeguarded.

(D) One of the Satanic designs of the great colonial and exploitative powers that has been in operation for long and in Iran and executed to the utmost and followed up by other means during the reign of Muhammad Reza Shah was to exclude the religious class from the social life. During Reza Khan's times they were pressurized and oppressed, sometimes disrobed, imprisoned and exiled, dishonored and executed and subjected to atrocities like that. During Muhammad Reza's times the same policy was pursued but with other means and methods. One of them was the creation of enmity between the university-educated and the *madarsa*-educated (theological students). A propaganda campaign was launched to this end. Unfortunately, because both the strata were unaware of the Satanic designs of the great powers it produced substantial results. On the one hand, effort was made to see to it that school and university teachers were selected and employed from among the westernized class or the Marxists alienated from Islam and all religions and the believers were reduced to a minority. These people were to train the influential section of the society from infancy to adolescence and youth to take up jobs in the government in the future in such a way that they developed an attitude of hatred towards all religions, particularly Islam, and the religious teachers and preachers. The latter were attacked in those days as agents of the British, supporters of capitalists and landlords and reactionaries and opponents of civilization and progress. On the other hand, they frightened the clergymen and preachers and the religious class of the university-educated class whom they accused of being irreligious, morally corrupt and opposed to all manifestations of religion. The aim was to antagonize the masses against the state and government and whatever was associated with them. This acute conflict between the university-educated and the seminary-educated made it easy for the plunderers to monopolise the state affairs and pocket the revenues of the state. So you see what happened to this nation. Now with God's will and nation's struggles all classes from clergymen to university-educated and the seminary-educated, the bazaaris, the workers and farmers and all the rest have broken loose of bondage, brought down the power-structure of the great powers and delivered the nation from their and their agents' stranglehold. I advise the present and future generations not to be complacent and the university-educated brilliant youth so far as possible should establish firmer and wider relations of friendship and understanding with the religious students and the clergy to thwart the designs and intrigues of the treacherous enemy. If anybody or group is found sowing seeds of discord between the two they should be counseled and set right. If it doesn't work they should be boycotted and isolated and not allowed to indulge in their intrigues as it is easy to plug the source. Especially if someone from among the professors creates dissensions he should be set right; if he does not mend his classes should be boycotted. This advice is addressed more to the clergymen and the seminary-educated. As intrigues in the universities deepen so it becomes the duty of the honorable sections who are the brains of the society to exercise surveillance over them.

(E) Of all designs one that has affected greatly other countries and our country too and is still in operation is to make the colonial people forsake their own national identities and become either westernized or easternized. So they despise themselves and their culture, belittle their national potential and regard the two power-poles of the west and east as superior races and cultures and dependence on one of them as an unavoidable obligation. The more saddening is the fact that the two keep the countries under their domination backward and consumption-oriented. They have so overawed us of their advances and their Satanic might that we have no courage to make any innovation. We surrendered everything to them and placed our and our country's destiny into their hands and with blind eyes and folded hands obeyed their commands. This artificial self-effacement and brainlessness became a cause for us not to rely on our own thinking and wisdom in any matter and to follow blindly either the west or the east. Moreover, the westernized or easternized writers and speakers denigrated our native culture, literature, industry, and inventions and made fun of them. They discouraged and suppressed native thinking and potential and are still doing so.

They popularized alien names and etiquettes, and manners of speech and writing, howsoever vulgar and unseemly, by praising them and advising the nation to assimilate them. For instance, if in a book or article or speech a few foreign words and phrases were used the writer or speaker was applauded as a great thinker or speaker without looking at the content. Everything from the cradle to the grave given western or eastern name was praiseworthy and a manifestation of civilization and progress. But if they bore native names were regarded as avoidable, old-fashioned and reactionary. If our children had western names they were to be proud but if they bore native names they were to lower their heads and take a back seat. If the avenues, streets, stores, companies, drugstores, libraries, costumes and other items, had foreign titles they became attractive and popular. Westernization from head to toe in manners and social customs and all affairs of the society was a source of self-esteem, civilization, progress and advancement. Conversely, native customs and manners were treated as traditionalism and backwardness. For each illness or sloth though curable at home one proceeded abroad and deprecated and disappointed the native doctors and physicians.

Going to Britain, France, the USA and Russia was a source of pride but pilgrimage to Mecca and other religious shrines was traditionalism and backwardness. I don't claim that we have everything available with us.

It is known that throughout history, particularly during the last few centuries they (foreign powers) deprived us of all advancements. The treacherous politicians, particularly of the Pahlavi regime and their propaganda organs, demeaned us by belittling everything native and the native achievements and thus they undermined our dynamism for advancement.

Goods of all varieties were imported, young men and women encouraged to use imported items like beauty products, luxury goods and children's toys, and households were drawn to competition in acquisition of consumer goods. This was a sad story. The youth were drawn to depravity by establishing centres of obscenity and entertainment and tens of other such hazards. There were calculated moves to keep these countries backward. I humbly beseech my countrymen to see that now that you have freed yourselves largely from these traps the present deprived generation has risen to activity and creativity. Formerly, it was unthinkable that Iranian experts would be able to create and operate factories to produce sophisticated goods like aircraft but now they are capable of doing so. We had to look towards the west or the east for experts to come and launch the projects for us. In the wake of economic sanctions and Iraq-imposed war our young people themselves manufactured the required spare parts and made them available at cheap prices and thus they proved that if we are determined we can achieve anything.

Keep vigil, beware, and watch out that the politicians connected with either the west or the east do not draw you by their Satanic designs towards any one of these international plunderers and with determined will, dynamism and self-reliance rise up to do away with these dependencies. You must know that the Aryan and Arab race is by no means inferior to the European or American or Russian race. If you realize yourselves and overcome pessimism and don't look towards other, you may acquire the capacity to do anything and manufacturing anything in the long run. Whatever these people have achieved you can also achieve provided you trust in God, rely on yourselves, terminate dependence on others and bear hardship to attain a life of honour free from the domination of foreigners.

It is incumbent upon states and their functionaries, whether of the present or the future, to pay due regard to their own experts and encourage them to work by providing them material and intellectual incentives and desist from importing consumer and nation-destroying goods. They should utilize their own resources to make things which they can make. I want the young men, daughters and sons not to sacrifice their independence, freedom and human dignity, even if they face some inconvenience or hardship over luxuries, pleasures, moral laxity or visiting centres of obscenity created for you by the west and its anti-national agents. As experience has shown, they are concerned with nothing but your ruin and making you indifferent to the destiny of your country, plundering your natural resources, subjecting you to colonial domination, making your nation consumption-oriented and stamping the stigma of dependence upon you. With these means they desire to keep you in a state of backwardness or 'semi-savagery' as they describe it.

(F) One of their big intrigues pointed out earlier and recalled here is the control of centers of education and training, particularly the universities, whose products are the custodians of destinies of nations. Their attitude towards the religious class and religious seminaries differs from their attitude towards the universities and secondary schools. They aimed at marginalizing and isolating the clergymen, either by means of coercion, violence and humiliation as practised during Reza Khan's times which produced the opposite results or by propaganda and defamation and the Satanic designs to separate the modern educated class called the intellectuals from the religious class and this was also implemented simultaneously with the pressurization and penalization of the clergy as practised under Reza Khan and continued by Muhammad Reza through violence but with more ferocity. So far as the universities were concerned, they alienated the youth from their own culture, literature and norms and drew them either to the west or the east. They chose the rulers from this class and entrusted them with the destinies of their nations that they would execute what was required of them. These people were instrumental in the plundering and westernization of their country. The religious class because it was marginalized isolated and broken down could do nothing to halt it.

This was the best course to plunder the dependent countries and to keep them backward. For the great powers without any effort and spending money drew everything of these nations into their pockets. Now that the universities are undergoing reform and purge we are all bound to extend our support to the authorities and should never allow the universities to be drawn to deviation. If deviation is seen anywhere it should be eliminated as soon as possible. This vital matter should be settled by the strong hands of the young men of universities and academies, for the emancipation of the universities from deviation is tantamount to the emancipation of the entire state and nation.

And I advise the young men first, fathers mothers and their well-wishers second, then the statesmen and the intellectuals that in this crucial effort that protects your country from all troubles, act devotedly and diligently and hand over (reformed) universities to the future generations.

I advise all the coming generations that for the sake of their own emancipation and their country's preservation of man-making Islam to guard and protect the universities against deviation and westernization and easternization. With this human and Islamic mission of your cut out the hands of the great powers from your country and disappoint them. May God help and protect you.

(G) An important issue is the commitment on the part of the deputies of the *Majlis-i-Shoora-i-Islami* (parliament). We have seen what saddening assaults were made against Islam and the Iranian state by a corrupt and deviant Majlis since the Constitutional Revolution, till the advent of the criminal Pahlavi regime and worse and more dangerous than any other age. It was a corrupt and petty regime and the normless servile criminals inflicted grievous sufferings and crippling losses upon the state and nation. During the last 50 years a deviant trumped up parliamentary majority as opposed to an oppressed minority was instrumental in the execution of the designs of Britain, Russia and later the USA through these God-forgetting deviant deputies who led the country to death and destruction.

In the aftermath of the Constitutional Revolution none of the substantive articles of the Constitution were ever observed. Before Reza Khan the ascendancy of the westernized elite and Mushti Khan and the landlords and during the Pahlavi era the bloody regime and its agents were responsible for it.

Now that with the grace of God and courage of the noble nation the destiny of the nation is entrusted to the people, deputies elected by them without the interference of the state agents and the *khans* (landlords) in the provinces, take their seats in the Majlis. It is hoped with their commitment to Islamic ordinances and interests of the country there will be no deviation from the right path. My advice to the nation in the present and future is that with your firm determination and commitment to Islamic norms and national interests choose deputies who are committed to Islam and the Islamic Republic and possibly those belonging to the middle class and to the downtrodden class. They should not deviate from the right path to embrace either the west or the deviant ideology of the east. They should send to the Majlis educated persons well-informed of the issues of the day and Islamic norms. I advise the honorable clergymen, particularly the exalted sources of emulation (*maraje'*), to engage themselves in the problems of the society particularly in such matters as election of the President of the Republic and deputies of the Majlis. They should not keep aloof from nor remain indifferent to them. You have seen and the future generations shall read that the clergy who (in 1906) laid the foundations of constitutional rule by their toils were later excluded from the political arena by the westernized lot. The clergy too fell into this trap as they themselves saw any involvement in political activities as beyond their sphere of activity and thus left the field entirely to the westernized intellectuals and thereby brought such consequences to constitutionalism, the constitution and Islam which require a long time to recompensate.

Now praise be to God that when all obstacles have been removed and the field is clear for the participation of all strata there is no excuse for and it will be an unpardonable sin to neglect the affairs of the Muslims. Everybody must serve Islam and the homeland within his power and influence and must prevent the infiltration of the allies of two imperialist power-blocs, of the westernized and easternized lot, and those who deviated from the noble ideology of Islam. They must know that enemies of Islam and Islamic states are the very same international plunderers – the superpowers – who by gradual and subtle steps want to create chaos in our country and other Islamic countries through our own countrymen so as to draw them into the trap of their exploitation. You must be watchful and consciously take the first decisive step to encounter them and don't give them any respite. May God help and protect you.

From the representatives of the Majlis of this era and the coming eras I want this. If God unwilling some deviant elements find their way to the Majlis through manipulation the Majlis should reject their credentials and should not allow even a single disruptive person to enter the Majlis. To the officially recognized religious minorities my advice is to take a lesson from the Pahlavi era and elect their representatives from among persons who are committed to their own religion and to the Islamic Republic having no link with the world-devouring powers and without a leaning to the atheist or eclectic schools. I want all representatives to work in unison and in good faith and fraternal spirit and see to it that no law contrary to Islam is passed by the Majlis. All must be loyal to Islam and its heavenly ordinances so that you attain success in this world and the world hereafter. I advise the honorable Guardian Council of the present and the future to perform their Islamic function carefully and to the best of their ability and should not let themselves be influenced by any power. They should set aside without any consideration any law found contrary to the holy *shariat* or the Fundamental Law. They should pay attention to the requirements of the state which sometimes can be met with secondary rules and sometimes by the Supreme Leader (*Valiyy-i-Faqih*) directly.

My advice to the noble nation is that in all elections whether of the President of the Republic or the representatives of the Majlis or the Assembly of Experts for the choice of the Leader or the Leadership Council [the provision for a Leadership Council was deleted from the Constitution in 1989] to participate actively and elect persons according to rules so that elections are credible. If they are negligent and elect the experts not strictly in accordance with religious and legal norms they will likely inflict irreparable damage to Islam and the country. In this case all shall be accountable before God. Similarly for non-participation of the nation the exalted sources of emulation, the great theologians, bazaaris, farmers, workers and technicians all will be accountable for the fate of the country and Islam. Often non-participation or negligence on certain occasions may be tantamount to the commitment of a great sin.

So an event must be tackled on its occurrence; otherwise, the matter will slip out of the hands. This is a fact which you and we have experienced ever since the Constitutional era. For no remedy is better than this that in the performance of functions entrusted to them the people throughout the country must act in accordance with Islamic norms and the Fundamental Law. In the choice of the President of the Republic and the deputies of the Majlis they must consult with educated persons who are committed, enlightened and well-versed in public affairs having no link with exploiting powers. They should also consult with the theologians and clergymen pious and committed to the Islamic Republic. They must ensure that the President of the Republic and the deputies of the Majlis should be from a class that is familiar with the deprivation and destitution of the downtrodden and the deprived of the society and ready to devote themselves to their well-being, and not from a class of capitalists, land-devourers and affluent notables submerged in the enjoyment of good things and satisfaction of bodily appetites, incapable of feeling the cruelty of deprivation and the hardships of the hungry and the barefooted.

And we must know that if the President of the Republic and the representatives of the Majlis are decent men committed to Islam no difficulty is likely to arise. Even if one arises it may be dealt with smoothly. Similarly due importance should be given to the election of the Assembly of Experts for the choice of the Leader or the Leadership Council. If experts elected by the people with due care and in consultation with the exalted sources of emulation, great theologians and men of knowledge go to the Assembly of Experts no difficulty is likely to arise in the choice of the Leader or the Leadership Council. Even if some difficulty arose it may be tackled decently. A reference to Articles 109 and 110 will show how crucial is the function of the nation in the choice of the Leader. A minor oversight in the choice may inflict such harm on Islam and the country and the Islamic Republic which would be beyond imagination. This makes their function of choice a divine obligation.

I advise the leader and the Leadership Council that this era is an era of an offensive of the superpowers and their external and internal allies against the Islamic Republic. It is in fact an offensive against Islam. His duty as the head of the Islamic Republic in the coming ages is that he should devote himself to the service of Islam and the deprived and the downtrodden and should never think that leadership for him is a gift or high office. It is rather an extraordinary and crucial duty. If they commit even a minor error because of their selfish desires they will earn eternal condemnation in this world and the wrath of God in the world hereafter. I humbly pray to God that in this test He may admit you and us in his presence and grant us His mercy. This risk also exists for the President of the Republic of the present and the future and governments and functionaries according to their rank and responsibility. They should regard God Almighty as omnipresent and overseeing and always deem themselves to be in his presence. May God open up their path.

(H) The judicial function is a crucial matter which concerns the life, property and honor of the people. I advise the Leader and the Leadership Council that in the choice of the highest judicial personnel which is in their jurisdiction they should try to appoint a committed person with good antecedents and well-versed in religious and political matters. I want the Supreme Judicial Council [abolished by a constitutional amendment in 1989 and its functions transferred to the President of the Judicial Power] to restructure the judicial system which was in a shambles under the former regime. The judges who play with the life and property of the people and whose objective is not the dispensation of Islamic justice should be remove form their judicial posts. The judiciary should be transformed gradually. God willing, judges possessing the requisite qualifications will be educated and trained in the religious seminaries of Qum who will replace the judges who are not familiar with the Islamic Law. In this way, God willing, Islamic justice shall prevail throughout the country. My advice to the honorable judges of the present and future ages is that they should occupy their posts with due regard to traditions of the infallible Imams regarding the enormity of adjudication and justice. They should also mind what has been said about unjust judgments. This function should not be assigned to the incompetent persons nor competent persons should refrain from discharging it so as not to leave the field open for the incompetent. They must know that just as the risks of this profession are great so its compensation and reward too are great. They must know that dispensation of justice for those who are competent to assume is a *farz-i-kifaya* [an optional communal obligation].

(I) My advice to the complex of the religious seminaries (*hauza-i-ilmiyya*), which I have offered repeatedly, is that in this era the enemies of Islam have aimed at uprooting Islam and tried to achieve this objective by all possible means. One important method to achieve their objective is to make deviant and subversive elements infiltrate the seminaries which is dangerous for Islam and the *hauza*. In the short run it produces the great risk of defamation of these seminaries on account of their indecent and deviant behaviour. But the greater danger in the long run is that may be one or more of such cunning persons after gaining mastery in Islamic sciences occupy high posts and gather influence among the innocent people. Then they may lie in wait for a proper opportunity to launch a fatal attack against religious seminaries and Islam. We already know that the plundering great powers plant amidst societies such persons in different garbs like nationalists, fake liberals, and pseudo-clergymen who become a danger greater than anything and inflict harm at proper moment. Some body lives patiently among the people for thirty or forty years as a holy man or a pan-Iranist or a nationalist and then performs his appointed task at a proper time. Our nation in this short period after the (1979) revolution has seen some such types such as *Mojahideen-i-Khalq* or *Fida'iyy-i-Khalq* or *Tudeh* and what not. We must counteract their intrigues in all alertness.

More important than anything else is the reorganization and purging of these seminaries with the concurrence of the sources of emulation and help of the honorable teachers and graduates. Perhaps the thesis of "order in disorder" has been inspired by these wicked plotters and intriguers. At any rate, my advice is that in all ages, particularly the present age in which the plots and intrigues have assumed ferocity and speed, it is essential and indispensable to reorganize the seminaries. The theologians and the graduates should spare their time and by formulating perfect plans should protect the seminaries, particularly those at Qum, from all harm. It is essential that the theologians and teachers in their lectures on jurisprudence should not depart from the approach of the predecessors to Islamic jurisprudence. They should strive to engage in daily discussions and conduct researches so that classical jurisprudence a legacy of our righteous predecessors, is preserved and researches added upon researches. But in other disciplines plans may be devised which are appropriate to the needs of the country, Islam and the persons trained in them. Of the highest and most valuable subjects that must be taught generally are Islamic ethics, self-purification, biographies of righteous people and Islamic theosophy. That may be regarded as *Jihad-i-Akbar* [greatest struggle].

Of matters that call attention is the purging of and surveillance over the executive branch. It may be that sometimes the Majlis passes a law that is progressive and beneficial for the society, the Guardian Council clears it and the minister concerned transmits it to the appropriate levels for implementation. But it falls into the hands of corrupt officials who distort it or act against the rules or indulge in red-tapism and delaying tactics that has become their habit or deliberately harm the people so that the people become desperate and prepare for revolt.

(J) My advice to responsible ministers in this and the coming ages is that not only you but all public servants get their livelihood out of the public budget whose revenues are paid by the people so it is people's money. So you must be the servants of particularly the downtrodden people, and take trouble for their sake. Action contrary to your duties is *haraam* (forbidden) and God unwilling, may invite divine wrath. All of you need nation's support. We succeeded and tyrannical rule came to an end because we had the backing of the people, particularly the downtrodden people. If some day you lose their support you will be set aside and in your place will be installed lowly oppressors the like of the former monarchical regime. You must seek and maintain the support of the people and desist from inhuman and un-Islamic behaviour. With this view I advise the ministers of state to take pains in selecting the provincial governors. They should appoint only the competent, religious, committed, considerate persons familiar with the people so that peace prevails in the country as far as possible. It is understood that although all ministries are responsible for Islamization and ordering of affairs within their jurisdictions some have special responsibility like the foreign ministry which is responsible for maintaining embassies abroad. Ever since the triumph of the Islamic Revolution I have been reminding the foreign ministers to weed out the remnants of monarchical influence in the foreign ministry and convert the embassies into embassies compatible with the Islamic Republic. But some of them either did not agree with me or were unable to effect any positive change. Now that three years have passed since the Revolution the present foreign ministry has taken an initiative to this end and it is hoped that with necessary support and time consumed this important task will be accomplished.

My advice to the foreign ministers of the present and future is that your responsibility is very great, whether as regards the reformation and restructuring of the ministry and the embassies or in foreign policy or preservation of national sovereignty, promotion of national interests and maintenance of good relations with countries that do not intend to interfere in our domestic matters. If any matter smacks of dependence in any of its dimensions avoid it altogether. You must understand that dependence in certain respects may appear deceivingly attractive or may deliver some temporary benefits but ultimately it will cut at the roots of your nations. Try to improve relations with the Islamic states and awaken their statesmen and call them to unity and solidarity as God is with you

And my advice to the Islamic states is that don't expect that somebody from outside will come to help you to reach your goal of enforcing Islam and its ordinances. You have yourselves to undertake this vital task which makes sovereignty and freedom real. The religious scholars and sermon-deliverers of the Islamic countries must press their governments to get rid of dependence on foreign powers and come to an understanding with their own people. In this way they will meet with success. They should also call upon the nations to unite and avoid racial and ethnic feelings which are contrary to Islamic teachings. Of whatever race or ethnicity they may be extend to them the hand of brotherhood as the great Islam has designated all of you as brothers. If this brotherhood of faith comes into being some day with the determination of the people and states and divine support you would see the Muslims would constitute the greatest power on earth. We hope for the day this fraternity and equality prevails by the divine will.

My advice to the Ministry of Islamic Guidance of all ages, particularly the present age which has a special significance, is that please strive to propagate the right against the wrong and introduce the real face of the Islamic Republic. We that in this age eliminated the influence of the great powers from our country have become a target of the propaganda offensive of all the media attached to the great powers. What lies and false accusations against this new-born republic have not been leveled and are still not being made by writers and commentators attached to the great powers. It is regretted that most of the countries of the Islamic region which according to Islamic teachings must extend the hands of brotherhood to us have risen to oppose us and the Islamic Republic. And all have in the service of the world-devourers launched an offensive against us from all sides. Our propaganda capacity is limited. You must understand that the world today revolves around propaganda. Unfortunately the so-called "intellectual" men of letters inclined towards one of the two power-blocs do not think of the independence and freedom of their own country. Their selfishness, opportunism and monpolism do not allow them to think over a moment and take the interests of their country and nation into consideration. Let them compare the independence and freedom prevailing in the Islamic Republic with tyrannical regime of the past. Compare the honorable life which they lead now although bereft of something which they have lost, i.e. affluence and ostentatious life-style, with what they received from the tyrannical regime in lieu of sycophancy, servility, eulogizing and praising those creatures of corruption and mines of tyranny and obscenity. They attack this new-born republic with improper charges and accusations and with their pens and tongues assault a nation which stands unitedly against the tyrants and oppressors.

The problem of propaganda is not confined to the Ministry of Guidance only. It is an obligation of thinkers, speakers, writers and artists. The foreign ministry should see to it that embassies circulate publicity material which presents the shining face of Islam before the world. If this face of Islam is revealed in all that beauty to which Quran and traditions invite from behind the veil put upon it by its opponents and the misguided self-displaying friends of Islam, Islam will become a global religion and its banner will flutter everywhere. How saddening that Muslims have something precious the equal of which will not be found from the beginning till the end are not able to present it as every man of free nature seeks it. Instead they themselves are unaware and ignorant of it and sometimes escape from it.

(K) One of the most important and destiny-making matters concerns centers of education and training from the nurseries up to the universities that is reiterated here again for its extraordinary importance and I shall make only passing references. The ruined nation must know that what has struck a fatal blow to Islam during the past half a century has mainly come from the universities. If there were universities and other centres of education and training with Islamic and national programmes for the benefit of the country to educate and train the children, adolescents and the young men our homeland would never have fallen into the stranglehold of first Britain, then the USA and Russia and the anti-national agreements would never have been imposed upon the deprived and ruined nation and foreign advisers would never have set their feet on the Iranian soil and never would the natural resources and the black gold of the nation flown into the pockets of the Satanic powers and never would the Pahlavi dynasty have plundered the assets of the nation and built parks and villas at home and abroad over the bodies of the oppressed and fill the foreign banks with the product of the labour of these oppressed and spend their money on pursuit of pleasure for them and their henchmen. Had the Majlis, the government, the judiciary and other organs their origins in the Islamic and national universities our nation today would not have fallen to devastating difficulties. if pious persons with Islamic and national tendencies in the true sense were supplied by the universities to the three branches of government our condition today would have been its reverse and our homeland would have been other than what is today and our deprived people would have been freed of the bonds of deprivation and the complexes of tyranny and centres of obscenity and liquor and narcotics shops and the houses of pleasure all meant to destroy the young generation would not have existed. Had the universities been Islamic, humanistic and national they could have turned hundreds and thousands of teachers to the society. But unfortunately universities and schools were run by such persons and our children received instruction at the hands and of such persons who were, except a deprived minority, either westernized or easternized. They occupied the chairs in the universities with their mandated plans and programmes. Our children were forced to grow under the patronage of these wolves who were attached to the great powers and when later on they occupied their posts in the legislature, executive and the judiciary they had to act according to the command of the tyrannical Pahlavi regime. Now praise be to God the universities are freed form the stranglehold of these expelled criminals. It is for the people and the Islamic Republic to bar the entry of the corrupt elements into the universities, academies and other educational institutions. They should be checked at the first step so that no difficulty arises later and control is not lost. My advice to young men in academies, schools and universities is that they themselves confront the deviations bravely so that independence and freedom of themselves and their nation-state is safeguarded.

(L) The armed forces, namely the army, the Revolutionary Guards the *Basij* and the tribesmen possess a special significance. They are powerful arms and wings of the Islamic Republic who guard the frontiers, the roads and routes, the cities and the villages and ultimately safeguard peace and security of the nation. They should be an object of special attention of the Majlis and the government. It must be understood that in the world whatever is an object of exploitation by the great powers and a target of their subversive policies is more than anything else and more than any group the armed forces. It is the armed forces which are used in the political games of staging *coup d'etat* and toppling of governments and regimes. The cunning self-seekers buy some of their heads and in collusion with these commanders capture the state apparatus, bring the oppressed people under their domination and deprive them of their independence and freedom. If upright commanders are put at the helm of affairs never will there be a possibility of enemies staging a *coup d'etat or* occupying a country. If any such eventuality arises the faithful commanders can manage it.

In Iran also the miracle of the age has taken place at the hands of the people. The committed armed forces and faithful patriotic commanders have a big share in it. Today the war imposed on us by Saddam Takriti at the behest of the USA and other powers is witnessing during a couple of years political and military defeat of the aggressive Ba'ath army and their powerful allies and supporters. Again, the armed forces, police, paramilitary guards and volunteers, with full backing of the people on the front and behind the front have brought about this pride and made Iran lofty. Also the internal mischiefs and intrigues by the puppets of either the west or the east and employed to destroy the Islamic Republic were suppressed by the strong hands of the young men of the revolutionary committees, revolutionary guards, the *basij,* the *shahrbani* and the people. And these very young men keep vigil all night so that families sleep well. May God help them.

So my advice during these last days of mine for the armed forces generally is that O dear ones devote yourselves to Islam and longing to unite with God sacrifice yourselves on the front and carry on your useful work on various levels in the country. Be awake, beware as the political game-players and professional politicians of the west and east and the hidden hands of criminals under the cover are aiming at you with the sharp edge of the weapon of treachery. These criminals are having an eye on you, more than any other group and want to exploit you dear ones in topping the Islamic Republic, you who by your struggles made the Revolution successful and revived Islam. They want to separate you from Islam and the people and put you in the lap of one of the two power-poles and to cancel out your struggles and sacrifices by political gimmicks and Islamic and national appearances.

My emphatic advice to the armed forces is that as non-participation of the military in parties and groups has been ordained by military law follow it and never should an armed force whether army or police or guards or *Basij* join a political party but must keep aloof from the game of politics. Only in this way you can safeguard your military prowess and be immune from inter-party rivalries. It is incumbent upon the commanders to forbid their men from joining political parties. For the revolution was waged by the entire nation and it is the duty of all to protect it. It is the duty of nation-state, the Defence Council and the Majlis to see to it that if the armed forces, whether commanders or the higher echelons or the lower echelons, act against the interests of Islam and the country or join political parties that no doubt shall lead to destruction or engage in political activity they must be stopped at the very outset. It is for the Leader or the Leadership Council to rule out such activities categorically so that the country is safe from trouble. Towards the end of my earthly life I advise the armed forces that just as you are loyal to Islam today remain loyal to it consistently. It is the only school of independence and freedom to which God calls. So that it emancipates you and your nation from the dishonour of dependence on and attachment to powers that want nothing of you but to become their slaves and to keep your country dependent and an object of oppression. One must prefer a life of dignity with hardships to a life of slavery to foreigners though with animalistic well-being. Understand that so long as you go begging to others for your requirements of products of advanced technology and pass your lives in dependence you will never be able to invent or innovate. Look closely and realistically at the fact that during the short period since economic sanctions were imposed on Iran those very people who considered themselves incapable of manufacturing anything and had no hope of erecting factories gathered their thoughts and met all the requirements of the army and the factories. This war, the sanctions and exodus of foreign experts was a divine gift we were forgetful of. Now if the state and the army themselves ban the import of goods of the world-devourers and make an added effort towards research and development the country may be expected to become self-reliant and saved from begging the enemy.

Here I must add that our need for advanced technology of the west after all this artificial backwardness of ours is an undeniable fact. But this does not mean that we attach ourselves to one of power-blocs in search of science and technology.

The state and the army should send committed students to countries possessing advanced technology that are non-imperialist and non-exploitative and refrain from sending them to the USA and Russia and other countries which are allies of these two poles. God willing a day will come when these two powers themselves will realize their mistake and taking the path of humanism respect the rights of others. Or God willing the downtrodden of the world and awakened nations and committed Muslims will overtake them. Let us hope for that day to come.

(M) Radio, television, press, cinema and theatres are effective instruments for the ruination and dulling of people, particularly the youth. During the past 100 years, particularly the last half a century, these instruments played a big role in propagating against Islam and the clergy and were used for imperialistic propaganda, of the west and east. They were utilized for creating markets for their luxury goods and beauty products of all sorts and propularising the adoption of their architecture, decorations and luxuries and of their softdrinks and costumes. Being westernized in all respects whether manners, speech or dress was thought to be honorable. And this life-style was adopted by the affluent and semi-affluent ladies. Western manners were imitated in social intercourse, conversations and use of European words became a vogue which were incomprehensible to most people, even to their peers. Television films produced in the west or east were such that diverted the young men and women from the normal course of life, work, industry, production and pursuit of knowledge and made them forget their own identity and personality or to despise whatever was native even the culture, literature and invaluable antiquities most of which have now found their way to the museums and libraries of the west or east through the treacherous profit seekers.

Periodicals with articles and obscene photographs and daily newspapers running a race through articles against their own culture and against Islam proudly exhorted the people especially the active youth towards the west or the east. Add to them the centres of corruption, the pleasure houses, casinoes, lotteries, stores full of luxury goods, decorative items, toys and sport goods and alcoholic drinks particularly those imported from the west. Against revenues earned from the export of oil, gas and other minerals puppets, toys, luxury gift items were imported and there were hundreds of other items I am not aware of. If God unwilling, had the deposed self-destroying Pahlavi regime been in place the nation and Islam would have lost our brilliant youth, these children of Islam and the homeland who are the hope of our nation, through all sorts of intrigues and Satanic designs of the corrupt regime, the mass media and the westernized or easternized intellectuals attached to it.

Now my advice to the *Majlis-i-Shura-i-Islami* (the Islamic Consultative Assembly) of the present and the future and the President of the Republic and the coming presidents of the republic, to the Guardian Council and judiciary and governments of all ages is that don't allow these media and the newspapers and the periodicals to depart from the Islamic and national interests. We all must understand that freedom in its western sense that degrades our youth, sons and daughters is condemnable from the view of Islam and reason. All publicity, articles, speeches, books and periodicals contrary to Islam and public decency and state interests are *haraam* (forbidden) and it is obligatory upon us and all Muslims to stop them. All destructive freedom should be curtailed. Whatever is *haraam* in the eyes of the Islamic law and whatever is against national and state policy and all opposition to the foundations of the Islamic Republic if not checked absolutely all will be responsible (for the consequences). The people and the *hizbullahi* youth [the followers of Imam Khomeini] must report to the concerned agencies anything mentioned above and if those agencies do not act they must stop such things themselves. May God help you.

(N) My advice to groups, factions and individuals active against the nation, the Islamic Republic and Islam, first of all to their leaders at home and abroad, is that the long experience of what actions you took, what intrigues you indulged in and what states and authorities you sought aid from must have taught you, as you are yourselves knowing and understanding, that the course of a self-sacrificing people cannot be changed by a few acts of terrorism or bomb explosions or senseless and baseless lies. You can never topple a government with such irrational means, especially in Iran where all from minor children to the elderly men and women are struggling and making sacrifices for their goals, for the sake of the Republic and the Quran and the faith. You who understand well (and if you don't understand you are thinking like simpletons) that the nation is not with you and the army is your enemy and assuming that they were with you and your friends your vicious acts and the crimes committed at your behest have alienated them from you and you can do nothing more than making enemies. I sincerely advise you towards the end of my life that first you have risen to fight against a tyrannized and oppressed people who after 2500 years of oppressive rule have got freedom from the tyranny of the criminal Pahlavi regime and the world-devourers of the west and east by sacrificing their best children and you. How could the conscience of a man (how much wicked he may be) allow himself to behave like this towards his own homeland and people having no mercy for the children and the old. I exhort you to give up these useless and senseless activities and don't fall in the trap of the world-devourers. Wherever you are if you did not commit a crime (against the Islamic Republic) return to your homeland and to Islam and repent because God Almighty is forgiving. The Islamic Republic and the people, God willing, will forgive you. If you ever committed a crime then God has fixed its responsibility upon you. Return from the midway, repent and if you have courage take the punishment of God. Otherwise, wherever you are don't waste your time. It is better for you to engage in some other useful work. After this I advise their followers at home and abroad for what cause are you wasting your youth for those who are provenly servile to the world-devourers and executing their plans and have unknowingly fallen into their trap? For what cause are you betraying your own nation? You have become their playthings. If you are in Iran see with your own eyes that millions of people are loyal to the Islamic Republic and ready to make sacrifices for it. See with your own eyes that the government and the present regime is whole heartedly working to serve the people and the needy. Those who falsely claim to be *Khalqis, Mujahids* and *Fidayees* [reference is to the dissident groups] have stood for the enemity of the creatures of God and have exploited you the simple-minded sons and daughters in their cause of serving one of the two world-devouring power-poles. And they themselves are either living lavishly abroad in the lap of one of the two superpowers or lead an aristocratic life at home in some of their luxurious hideouts from where they direct their criminal activities and despatch you young men to the jaws of death.

I kind heartedly exhort you adolescents and youth at home and abroad to turn away from the wrong path and devote yourselves wholeheartedly to the service of the deprived of the society. Be united and be active for the independence and freedom of Iran so that the nation-state is saved from the evil of the enemies and all lead a life of dignity. For how long and for what purpose did you become subservient to persons who don't think except of their own benefit and under the protection of the big powers are fighting against their own people and sacrificing you for their wicked objectives and power-politics? Throughout these years you have seen the Revolution triumphant and their words do not match their deeds. Their claims are merely to deceive the pure hearted youth. Understand that you don't have any capacity to withstand the roaring flood of the nation and your activities have no impact but your own harm and wastage of your lives. I have discharged my responsibility of guidance towards you and hope that you will heed my advice which reaches you after my death and has no power-seeing motive. May God guide you and show you the straight path.

(O) My advice to the leftists like the communists, people's guerillas and the like left-oriented groups is that you who never got true knowledge of religion and particularly Islam from people who have correct knowledge of it for what cause you have persuaded yourselves to embrace an ideology that has failed in the world today. How is it that you have espoused a certain "ism" whose substance according to scholars is trivial?

What motive has forced you to want your country to become a satellite of Russia or China and wage war against your country in the name of friendship of people or strike against the oppressed people as a result of the conspiracies of and for the benefit of the foreigners? You have seen that from the very beginning of communism its proponents were and are the greater dictators, autocrats and monopolists than any other government in the world. How many nations under Russian domination which tried to speak for their people were wiped out of existence? The Russian Muslims and non-Muslims alike, have been reeling under the oppression of the Communist Party and are deprived of all freedom and live under worst choking dictatorship. Stalin, a shining figure of the Party, lived like aristocrats and displayed all that pomp and show. Now you self-conceited people are giving your lives for the love of such a system. The oppressed people of the USSR and its satellites like Afghanistan have lost their liberty because of their atrocities. You who claim to be the defenders of the people you commit acts of crime against them wherever you can. You wrongly declared the gentle people of Amol [a city in Mazandran Province in northern Iran] as your loyalists and deceived a large number of them to wage war against the Republic and lose their lives. What crimes have you not committed! You the supporters of the deprived want to bring the deprived and oppressed people of Iran under Soviet dictatorship. You are committing such crimes under the names of *Fidaiyeen-i-Khalq*. The same is being done by the Tudeh Party by intriguing under the mask of supporting the Islamic Republic and by other armed and terrorist groups.

I advise the parties and groups whether they are leftists – though there is evidence to believe that some of them are of American variety – or whether those who get their livelihood and inspiration from the west or whether they have taken up arms in the name of the autonomy of the Kurds and Baluchs and have caused the extermination of the deprived people of Kurdistan and other places and blocked the delivery of cultural, health, economic and reconstruction services of the Islamic Republic to these regions, like the Democratic Party or the Komoleh, to rejoin the nation. Until now they have seen that they have done nothing except to bring misfortune to the inhabitants of these regions and cannot do anything else. So you should mind the interests of yourselves, your nations, your region and join the national reconstruction effort and rest assured that Islam for you is a better alternative than the criminal west or the dictatorship pole of the east and best fulfills human aspirations.

And my advice to Muslim groups who mistakenly are inclined towards the west and sometimes towards the east and to the hypocrites whose treachery became known recently as sometimes they wrongly supported the opponents and ill-wishers of the Islamic Republic and sometimes they denounced them, is this that don't persist in your mistake and identify yourselves with the government, the Majlis and oppressed people for the pleasure of God and deliver these downtrodden of history from the domination of the arrogant mighty.

Remember the words of [Sayyid Hasan] Mudarres [a member of the Majlis who died in 1937] , an Islamic scholar of pious character and pure thought, which he spoke in the Majlis of his day: "If we have now to meet our doom why should we meet our doom with our own hands". I myself submit to you brothers-in-faith, in the memory of that martyr in the way of God, that if we are to be wiped out of existence at the hands of the criminal USA or the Soviets and meet our God with our honorable red blood it is better than to live an aristocratic life of affluence under the red banner of the east or the black banner of the west. This is the conduct and way of the prophets, the Imams and great men of religion. We must follow them. If we should convince ourselves that if a people wants to live their life without dependencies it can and no mighty power on earth can impose on them anything contrary to their own ideals. We must learn a lesson from Afghanistan. The usurping government and all the left parties were with the Soviets and still are but could not subdue the rebellious people.

In addition, the deprived people of the world today have awakened. It will not be long before this awakening leads to uprisings, movements and revolutions to get rid of the domination of the arrogant tyrants. And you Muslims who are committed to Islamic norms see the blessings of separation from both the west and the east. Native brains are busy in finding the path of self-reliance. Whatever the treacherous western experts once considered impossible for us has become possible today by virtue of the intellectual and manual capacity of the nations and state and more will be done in the long run. Unfortunately Revolution came very late. Had it occurred earlier under the dirty tyrannical monarchy of Muhammad Reza Iran would have been other than what it is today.

I advise the writer, speakers, intellectuals, the obstructionists and the complex-bearers that instead of wasting your time in opposition to the policies of the Islamic Republic and misusing your energy to think ill, wish ill, and speak ill of the Majlis, the government and all other functionaries and with this conduct of yours driving your country towards the spheres of the superpowers, make communion with your God one night, and if you don't believe in God, with your own conscience, and human beings are often unaware of it – and see on what criterion of justice have you ignored the blood of the youth killed on the front and in the cities. You have stood to wage a war of nerves against a nation which wants to get rid of domination of the oppressors and plunderers internal and external and preserve with self-sacrifice the independence and freedom which it got by sacrificing the lives of its children. You create dissensions, indulge in treacherous intrigues and plots and make way for the arrogant tyrants. Is it not proper to use your brain and pen and tongue to guide the government, the Majlis and the nation in the task of protection of the homeland? Is it not fit that you help the deprived and oppressed nation and consolidate the Islamic government with your support? Do you consider that this Majlis and the President of the Republic and the government and the Judiciary worse than those under the former regime? Have you forgotten the atrocities perpetrated by that damned regime upon this tyrannized nation? Don't you know that this Islamic country in those times, was a military base for the Americans and was treated like a colony or that all organs of government, the Majlis, the cabinet and the armed forces were under their control and what their advisers, technicians and experts did to this country and its resources? Have you forgotten the propagation of immodesty and obscenity throughout the country and the centres of corruption like brothels, casinos, pubs, liquor shops, cinemas and other such centres each being a great factor in the degeneration of the young generation? Have you ignored the media and the obscene magazines and dailies of that regime?

Now that nothing exists of those bazaars of corruption except that few courts or a few young people who might have infiltrated into the system from the ranks of the dissidents and may have committed certain bad acts to defame Islam and the Islamic Republic, or execution of some who were found guilty of "spreading corruption on earth" (*fasad-fil-ardh*) or waging war against Islam and the Islamic Republic? You cry out and join those who openly oppose Islam and the Islamic Republic and wage war against them by arms or pen and tongue which is fraternized with them whose blood is worth shedding who have become the light of your eyes and you sit among those jugglers who arranged the episode of 5 March and watched the fracas as spectators [reference is to the street clashes between the supporters of President Abol Hasan Bani Sadr and the *hizbullahis* on 5 March 1982]. The innocent youth were beat and injured. It is an Islamic and moral act and the duty of the executive and judicial authorities to sentence the opponents, the dissidents and the atheists to their doom but you cry out atrocities? I am sorry for some of you brothers-in-faith whose antecedents I know somewhat and some of you I have been in contact with but I am not sorry at all for those wicked persons in the garb of well-wishers and wolves under the cover of shepherds and the actors who made fun of everybody and were out to destroy the nation and the country and serve one of the two plundering power-poles. Those who with their dirty hands killed the accomplished youth and gentlemen and the theologians who cultivate the society and had no mercy for tyrannised Muslim children are hated by the society and damned by God Almighty. They have no chance of retreat as they are ruled by their Satanic souls. But you believing brothers why don't you serve the deprived and the downtrodden, men without food, cloth and shelter and aid them? Why do you complain? Have you compared the achievements of the Islamic Republic during the short period after the revolution despite the shortages, the imposed war and millions of internal and external refugees, and breaches of contract, with the developmental work of the former regime? Don't you know that development projects of that era were mostly confined to cities that too to the affluent sectors. The poor people had little or no share in these things. The present regime and the Islamic foundations are wholeheartedly serving this deprived section. You believers too support the government to speed up the development work so that when you do to the court of the Almighty where you have to go willy nilly, go there with a badge of service towards his creatures. (Here I have deleted some portion). One of the important objects worthy of reminding and counsel is that Islam is not compatible with callous and unbridled capitalism which keeps the masses deprived and oppressed. Such a system has been condemned in the Quran and the traditions of the Prophet and regarded as detrimental to social justice. But some misguided persons uniformed about the Islamic system of government and its principles have through their writings and speeches claimed that Islam advocates capitalism and private property without any limits. With this approach these misguided people have covered up the shining face of Islam and prepared the ground of its enemies and ill-wishers to claim that Islam too supports a western-style capitalist regime, as it exist in the USA, Britain and other plundering countries. Thus without learning about Islam from the real scholars of Islam and relying on naïve, motivated or stupid interpretations of Islam they have risen to oppose Islam. Nor Islam is like communism or a Marxist Leninist regime which abolishes private property and ordains collective ownership. With great variations from old times till now it even permits community of wives and homosexuality. It has created an omnipotent dictatorship. On the contrary Islam creates a moderate regime, recognizing the sanctity of private property under certain limits. If Islamic rules governing production and consumption are followed truly a healthy and sound economic system may come into being and social justice, a corollary of such a sound regime realized.

Then there is a second misguided group equally uniformed about true Islam and its economic principles which stands on the opposite side of the first group. The second group by citing certain verses form the holy Quran and certain passages from *Nihjul Balagha* declares islam to be compitable with the deviant school of Marxism Leninsm. They have arbitrarily school to support communism which ordains atheism, dictatorship, denial of human rights and subjection of a majority to a minority. My testimony to the Majlis and the Guardian Council, the President of the Republic and the judiciary is that you submit yourselves to the ordinances of God and don't be influenced by the baseless propaganda of either the plundering pole of capitalism or atheistic pole of communism. Respect private property and the legitimate capital within the Islamic limits. Assure the people to invest their capital for constructive purposes, to make the country self-reliant in light and heavy industries. I exhort the wealthy and monied class to deploy their legitimate wealth for productive purposes in farms, factories and villages as it is in itself a noble act of worship. I advise all to work for the welfare of the deprived classes. Your well-being in this world and in the world hereafter is bound with your concern for the condition of those downtrodden people who have suffered only hardship and misery throughout the history of *shahinshahi* (absolute monarchy) and *khan khani* (aristocracy) it would be an act of charity if the owning classes voluntarily provide amenities and construct housing for the shanty-dwellers and rest assured that this ensures well-being in this world and the world hereafter. It is contrary to justice that some people own apartments and some are without dwellings.

(P) My advice to that group of clergymen and pseudo-clergymen who oppose the Islamic Republic and its institutions from different motives and have reserved their time for toppling it, who receive money from the intriguing enemies and politicians and sometimes big money from the God-forgetting capitalist for this purpose, is this that you have not given up these wrongdoings of yours nor I suppose you will. It is better, as you have undertaken this mission for the sake of earning worldly gains God will not let you succeed in this wicked purpose of yours, to repent so long as the door of repentance is open. Seek the pardon of the Almighty. Come to the aid of the needy tyrannized people, and support the Islamic Republic which has been brought about by sacrifices of these people; for the well-being of this and the other world lies in it though I don't think that you will ever repent.

There is another group that because of certain mistakes committed advertently or inadvertently by certain persons or groups.

Connected with the regime that were contrary to the Islamic norms, oppose the Islamic Republic and its governmental system and work for its downfall as in their opinion this regime is worse than or equal to the former regime. They should ponder in their privacy in all earnestness and compare fairly this government with the former regime and then think again that during all revolutions disturbances, dislocations, wrongdoings and opportunistic acts are common and unavoidable. If you pay attention and take into account the difficulties of this Republic like conspiracies, false propaganda against it, armed attacks from without the frontiers and from within, uncheckable infiltration of groups of mischief-makers and opponents of Islam in all organs of the state with a view to alienating the people from Islam and the Islamic government; and the in experience of most state functionaries and circulation of false rumours by those who were barred from making illicit gains or whose gains had diminished; the shortage of religious judges; the back-breaking economic difficulties; the complexities of reforming and purging the million-strong employee force; and the shortage of upright and efficient experts these and lens of other difficulties cannot be grasped unless actually faced. On the other hand, selfish capitalists of the royalist camp who by their usury, profiteering, smuggling out of foreign exchange, hiking of prices, smuggling in of goods and hoarding of commodities pressed the poor people to the level of starvation and let the society to penury, come to you with their grievances and fabrications. Sometimes they prove that they are true Muslims by offering some money as *sahm* [the share of the Hidden Imam] and then shed crocodile's tears to provoke you to opposing us. Most of them suck the blood of the people by unfair means and subvert the economy of the country. I humbly offer my brotherly advice to you not to be misled by these rumours and strengthen the Republic for the sake of God and protection of Islam. You must know that if the Republic goes down it will not be replaced by an Islamic Republic of Hidden Imam's liking or a republic obedient to you gentlemen but by a regime of the liking of one of the two superpowers will be in place. Then the deprived people of the world who have high hopes of the Islamic Republic would be disappointed and Islam would go down for ever. That day you would repent for your misdeed. But after the damage is done your repentance will be of no avail. If you gentlemen desire that all affairs can be set right in accordance with Islamic principles overnight you are mistaken. During the whole of human history such miracles have not happened nor will they. The day, God willing, the Absolute Reformer [the Hidden Imam] return to the world don't think a miracle will happen and the world will get transformed in one day. But through struggles and sacrifices the tyrants will be defeated and suppressed. But if like the misguided vulgar people you too believe that to facilitate his return His Holiness will first see to it that the world is full of injustice to the brim so that the ground of his return is prepared then "We are for God and to God shall we return".

(Q) My advice to all Muslims and the downtrodden of the world is that you should not sit idle and expect that the rulers and functionaries of the country or foreign powers will come and deliver you the gift of independence and freedom. During at least the past 100 years we and you have observed that the world-devouring powers have gradually effected their domination of all the Islamic countries and the small countries [of the Third World]. The correct history tells us that governments ruling over these countries were never concern with independence, freedom or well-being of their own people nor they still are. Their majority has indulged in oppressing and strangulating these people. Whatever they do is for their personal or group interest or for the affluent upper strata and the downtrodden class living in shanties and pits has been deprived of all basic necessities even the drinking water and the daily bread. These unfortunate people are hired by the rich and the well-to-do. Or else these governments are installed by the great powers who do everything in their power to make who do everything in their power to make these countries dependent on them. They employ all the means to convert them into markets for the west or the east and to subvert their interests. They make them consumption-oriented societies and keep them backward. They are still active in implementing their plans. O you downtrodden of the world and O Islamic states and Muslims of the world stand on your own feet and stick to you own rights and don't be afraid of the propaganda noise of the great powers and their lackeys and depose the criminal rulers who surrender of yours and of Islam. With the help of the committed service class take over the reins of governments into your own hands and unite under the lofty banner of Islam and stand to defend the deprived of the world from the enemies of Islam and advance towards a (unified) Islamic state composed of all the independent and free republics. The realization of it will make the arrogant powers retreat and all the downtrodden lead and inherit the earth. We hope for the day promised by God Almighty.

(R) Towards the end of this testament I once again remind the noble people of Iran that in the world the volume of toils, sufferings, sacrifices, self-abnegation and deprivations is commensurate with the lofty and sublime goals pursued. Whatever you noble people of Iran stood for and still stand, for which you sacrificed your lives and property and are still doing so is the supreme noble goal from the beginning of the world will the eternity. That is the divine ideology in its broadest sense and the idea of monotheism with its lofty dimensions, the reason and the objective of whose creation permeates the depth of existence whether creation permeates the depth of existence whether visible or invisible. This has been revealed through the religion and faith of the Prophet Muhammad (peace be on him). All prophets and all great men of religion have strived to realize it. Without it nobody can attain to absolute excellence and boundless grandeur and beauty. It is what makes earthly beings superior to celestial beings. And what the earthly beings can achieve through practicing it cannot be achieved by any other creature openly or secretly.

You O struggling people are marching under a banner which is fluttering throughout the material and spiritual realm. Whether you find it or not, the path you are marching on is the path of all the prophets and is the only path of absolute salvation. This is the objective to attain which all men of God seek martyrdom and consider the red-blooded death sweeter than honey. Your young men have taken a sip of its on the front and are in a state of trance; it is manifest in mothers, fathers, brothers and sisters and we might rightly say: "Wish we were with you so we could also have attained the great success", Blessed be those who breathe the scintillating breeze and experience the glitter of divine reflection. Part of this glitter may be seen in farms, factories, workshops, centres of science and technology, in the people busy in bazaars, streets, villages and all those engaged in the service of Islam, the Islamic Republic and for the progress and self-reliance of the country. So long as this spirit of cooperation and commitment persists in the society our beloved country shall safe all troubles of the times. Praise be to God, the religious seminaries, the universities and the dear young men in the centres of education and training are blessed with this invisible divine inspiration. All these centres are in their control.

God willing, the subversives and the dissidents shall not find their way to them again.

My advice to all is to move forward remembering God towards the goal of self-realization, self-reliance and independence in all its dimensions. No doubt God's hand is with you, provided you are in his service and continue to work in a cooperative spirit for the progress and excellence of this Islamic country. And whatever awakening, alertness, commitment, self-sacrificing, spirit of resistance and perseverance in the path of Right (*haqq*) I see in my people I pray to God Almighty that they be transmitted to the coming generations and be added upon generation after generation. With a peaceful contented heart and a happy spirit and conscience full of hope of God's grace I take leave from the service of you sisters and brothers and prepare for my journey to my eternal abode. I pray to God to kindly accept my apologies for dereliction of my duties, and for acts of omission and commission. I request the people to accept my apology for all my shortcomings and acts of omission and commission.

They should move forward with all determination. You should know that departure of one servant does not make any dent in the iron gate of the nation as better and superior servants are available to this nation for service. God is the guardian of this nation and the oppressed of the world.

Ruhullah al- Musavi al-Khomeini

Peace be on you

.20 Bahman 1361 HS
15 February 1982

AFTER my death this testament should be read to the people by Ahmad Khomeini. In case of an excuse the President of the Republic or the Speaker of the Majlis or the Chief Justice of the Supreme Court should take this trouble. Failing them, this trouble should be taken by one of the members of the Guardian Council.

Ruhullah al-Musavi al-Khomeini

As a postscript to the 29-page testament I wish to present certain points:

1. Now that I'm alive certain baseless statements have been attributed to me and may be their volume increases after my death. I therefore submit that whatever has been or is being attributed to me is not authentic unless it is in my voice or hand-script with my signatures as authenticated by experts or unless I myself have said something over the radio of the Islamic Republic.

2. Some persons during my life have claimed to have written some statements for me. I strongly refute this falsehood. Until now nobody except me has prepared my statements.

3. Of this category is the claim of certain persons that my journey to Paris was arranged through their medium. This is a lie. When I was denied enty into Kuwait I selected Paris in consultation with Ahmad for there was no possibility of entry

into Islamic states. They were under Shah's influence but Paris was free from it.

4. Myself during the revolutionary movement and the revolution acknowledged and praised certain individuals who misled me by their sycophancy and Islamic pretentions. Later I knew that I had failed to understand their deception. I eulogized them when they were committed and loyal to the Islamic Republic. Such utterings should not be misused now. Everybody must be judged by his present standing.

Ruhullah al-Musavi al-Khomeini

Selected Bibliography

Abrahamian, Ervand, *Iran between the Two Revolutions* (Princeton: Princeton University Press, 1982).

_____, *Khomeinism.* Essays on the Islamic Republic (Berkeley: University of California Press, 1993.

Akhavi, Shahrough, *Religion and Politic in Iran* (New York: University of New York Press, 1980).

Algar, Hamid, *Religion and State in Iran* 1785-1906; the Role of the Ulama in the Qajar Period (Berkeley: University of California Press, 1969).

_____, *Islam and Revolution.* Writings and Declarations of Imam Khomeini (Berkeley: Mizan Press, 1981).

_____, *Roots of the Islamic Revolution in Iran* (Oneonta, NY: ICI, 2001).

Ali Khan, Hossein, *Sanctioning Iran.* Anatomy of a Failed Polity (London: I.B. Tauris, 2000).

Amjad, Mohammad, *Iran*: From Royal Dictatorship to Theocracy (New York: Greenwood Press, 1989).

Ansari, Ali M., *Modern Iran since 1921.* The Pahlavis and after (Harlow: Longman, 2003).

Arjomand, Said Amir, *From Nationalism to Revolutionary Islam* (Albany: State University of New York, 1983).

_____, *The Shadow of God and the Hidden Imam.* Religion, Political and Social Change in Shiite Iran from the beginning to 1890 (Chicago: University of Chicago Press, 1984).

_____, *The Turban for the Crown* (London: Oxford University Press, 1988).

_____, *Authority and Political Culture in Shiism* (Albany: State University of New York, 1988).

Bashiriyeh, H., *The State and Revolution in Iran* (London: Croom Helm, 1984).

Bharier, Julian, *Economic Development in Iran*, 1900-1970 (Oxford: Oxford University Press, 1971).

Bill, James A., *The Politics of Iran. Groups*, Classes and Modernization (Columbus, Ohio: Merrill, 1972).

_____, *Politics in the Middle East*, 3rd edition (London: Harper-Collins, 1990).

_____ and W.R. Louis, eds., *Musaddiq, Iranian Nationalism and Oil* (London: I.B. Taurus, 1989).

Cronin, Stephanie, *The Making of Modern Iran:* State and Society under Reza Shah (1921-1941). (London: Routledge Curzon, 2003).

Dekmejian, R.H. "The Anatomy of Islamic Revival: Legitimacy Crisis, Ethnic Conflict and the Search for Islamic Alternatives". *Middle East Journal* 3 (1980).

Eliash, Joseph, "Misconceptions regarding the Judicial Status of Iranian Ulama", *International Journal of Middle Eastern Studies* 10 (1979).

Enayat, Hamid, *Modern Islamic Political Thought* (Austin, Texas: University of Texas Press, 1982).

Esposito, John L. and R.K. Ramzani, *Iran at the Crossroads* (Basingsboke: palgrave, 2001).

Faghfoory, M.H., "The Impact of Modernization on the Ulama in Iran 1925-1941" *Iranian Studies* 21 (1993).

Farsoon, Samih K.; and Mehrdad Mashayekhi, *Iran*. Political Culture in the Islamic Republic (London: Routledge, 1993).

Floor, William M., "The Revolutionary Character of the Iranian Ulama: Wishful Thinking of Reality". *International Journal of Middle Eastern Studies*, 12 (1980).

Hairi, A.H., *Shiism and Constitutionalism in Iran* (Leiden: E.J. Brill, 1977).

Hidayati, Muhammad Ali, *Quww-i-Qazaiyya* [The Judicial Power] (Tehran: Hyderi, 1993).

Hoogland, Eric, *Twenty Years of Islamic Revolution:* Political and Social Transition in Iran since 1979 (Syracuse, NY: Syracuse University Press, 2002).

Katuzian, Homa, *The Political Economy of Iran* (New York: New York University Press, 1981).

_____, *Musaddeq and the Struggle for Power in Iran* (London: I.B. Tauris, 1990).

_____, *Iranian History and Politics* (Londong: Routledge Curzon, 2003).

Kawakabian, Mustafa, *Dimakrasi dar Nizam-i-Vilayat-i-Faqih* [Democracy under the Regime of Guardianship of the Jurisconsult] (Qum: Entesharaat-i-Islami, 1991).

Keddie, Nikki R., *Religion and Rebellion in Iran*: The Tobacco Protest of 1891-1892 (London: Frank Cass, 1966).

_____, *Iran: Religion, Politics and Society*. Collected Essays (London: Cass, 1980).

_____, ed., *Religion and Politics in Iran*: Shiism from Quietism to Revolution (London: Yale University Press, 1983).

_____, *Modern Iran*: Roots and Results of Revolution (New Haven/London: Yale University Press, 2003).

Kelidar, Abbas, "Ayattullah Khomeini's Concept of Islamic Government" *in Islam and Power*, ed., by A. Qudsi and Ali al-dessouiki (Baltimore, Md: The John Hopkins University Press, 1981).

Khomeini, Ruhullah Musavi, *Vilayat-i-Faqih.*Hukumat-i-Islami (Qum, 1976).

_____, *Dar Justuju-i-Rah az Kalam-i-Imam* [Collected Statements and Declarations of Imam Khomeini 1962-1982], 9 volumes (Tehran: Amir-i-Kabir, 1982).

_____, *Saheefa-i-Nur* [Collected Writings and Speeches of Imam Khomeini), 22 volumes (Tehran: Ministry of Culture and Islamic Guidance, 1982-1989).

_____, *Saheefa-i-Inquilab* [The Political Testment of Imam Khomeini, 1988] (Tehran, Zikr, 1995).

Lambton, Ann K.S., "The Impact of the West on Persia", *International Affairs* (1957).

Lenzowski, George, *Russia and the West in Iran* 1918-1948: A Study in Big-Power Rivalry (Ithaca: Cornell University Press, 1949).

Lockert, L., "The Constitutional Laws of Persia: an outline of their Origin and Development". *Middle East Journal* 13 (1959).

Looney, Robert E., *Economic Origins of the Islamic Revolution* (New York: the Pergamom Press, 1982).

Madani, S. Jalaluddin, *Huquq-i-Asaasi dar Jumhuriyy-i-Islamiyy-i-Iran* [The Constitutional Law of the Islamic Republic of Iran]. 7 volumes (Tehran: Sarosh, 1981-1991).

Marschall, Jones Christin, *Iran's Persian Gulf Policy:* From Khomeini to Khatami (London. Routledge Curzon, 2003).

Martin, Vanessa, *Islam and Modernism.* The Iranian Revolution of 1906 (London: I.B. Tauris, 1989).

_____, *Creating an Islamic State*: Khomeini and the Making of a New Iran (London: I.B. Tauris, 2001).

Menashri, David, *Post-Revolutionary Politics in Iran.* Religion, Society, Power (London: Cass, 2001).

Milani, Muhsin, *The Making of Iran's Islamic Revolution From Monarcy to the Islamic Republic* (London: Westview Press, 1988).

Miller, W.G,. "Political Organization in Iran: From Dowreh to Political Party", *Middle East Journal* 23 (1969).

Mortimer, Edward, *Faith and Power*. The Politics of Islam (NY, NY: Vintage Books, 1982).

Mottahedeh, Roy P., *The Mantle of the Prophet*. Religion and Politics in Iran (NY: Penguin Books, 1987).

Mousavi, A.K., "The Establishment of the Position of *Marja'iyyat-i-Taqlid* in the twelver Shii Community", *Iranian Studies*, 28 (1985).

Parsa, Misagh, *Social Origins of the Iranian Revolution* (New Brunswick / London: Rutgers University Press, 1989).

Rahimi, Mustafa, *Qanun-i-Asaasi dar Iran wa Usul-i-Dimakrasi* [The Law of the Constitution and Principles of Democracy in Iran] (Tehran: Sipah, 1969).

Ramzani, R.K., *Iran's Foreign Policy 1941-1973*. A Study of Foreign Policy in Modernizing Nations (Charlottsville: University Press of Virginia, 1975).

_____, *Revolutionary Iran*. Challenge and Response in the Middle East (Baltimore, Md.: The John Hopkins University Press, 1986).

_____,ed.,*Iran's Revolution*. The Search for Consensus (Bloomington, Indiana: Indiana University Press, 1990).

Sachedina, A.A., *Islamic Messianism* (Albany: State University of New York Press, 1980).

_____, The Just Ruler in Shiite Islam (Oxford: Oxford University Press, 1988).

Shahabi, H.E., *Iranian Politics and Religious Modernization*. The Liberation Movement under the Shah and Khomeini (Ithaca: Cornell University Press, 1990),

Upton, Joseph M., *The History of Modern Iran*. An Interpretation (Havard: Havard University Press, 1960).

Index

A

Ahmad Shah Qajar, 7
Ali Quli Khan, 4
Armed Forces, 86
Assembly of Experts on Leadership, 62 ff

B

Bani Sadr, Abol Hasan, 5
Basij (Volunteers), 87
Bazargan Mahdi,11ff
Board for Identifying the Expediency of the System, 78-79

C

Constitutional Revolution, 1906, 13, 15
Constitution of 1906/07, 50-56
Constitution of 1979, 121-188

F

Fidayeen-i-Khalq, 13, 66

G

Guardian Class, 31-46
Guardian Council, 74-75

H

Hidden Imam, 16, 23

I

Ijtihad and Mujtahid, 37-46
Imamat, 19 ff
Iran-Iraq War, 1980-88, 9
Iron Side, General Edmond, 5
Islamic Consultative Assembly, 80 ff, 152 ff
Islamic Republican Party, 4, 13, 79

J

Judiciary, 89-101

K

Khamenei, Ayatullah Sayyid Ali, 8, 11, 12, 25
Khomeini, Ayatullah Ruhullah Musavi, 8, 11, 25 ff

L

Leader (*Rahbar*), 59-66
Local Consultative Councils, 78

M

Majlis-i-Shura-i-Milli–See National Consultative Assembly *Majlis-i-Shura-i Islami* – See Islamic Consultative Assembly
Marja'iyyat, 19 ff
Mojahiddeen-i-Khalq, 13,66
Mohammad Ali Shah Qajar, 2 ff
Muhammad Musaddeq, 7 ff
Muhammad Reza Pahlavi, 20-23
Muntazeri, Ayatullah Hussein Ali,10

N

National Consultative Assembly, 3 ff, 55
National Freedom Movement, 66
National Front, 7, 66
National Security Council, 85
National Supreme Court, 55-61
Nationalization of Oil Industry, 1951, 1 ff

O

Occupation of American Embassy, 1979, 7, 12

P

Parliamentary Standing Commissions, 72
Pasdarans – See Revolutionary Guards,
Political Parties, 97 ff
Popular Referendums, 79
President of the Judicial Power, 92 ff
President of the Republic, 81-84
Presidential Cabinet, 84
Provisional Government, 1979, 13

R

Rafsanjani, Ali Akbar Hashmi, 12, 78
Revolution of 1979, 23-29
Revolutionary Council, 1979, 10
Revolutionary Courts, 93
Revolutionary Guards, 84
Revolutionary Prosecutors, 93
Reza Khan, 5, 6, 7, 18-20

S

SAVAK, 56-57
SAVAM, 56-57
Separation of Powers, 50
Shiism as State Religion, 15, 19, 36, 49, 128-134
Speaker of the Majlis, 69
State Investigation Organization, 95

T

Tabatabai, Ziauddin, 5
Tudeh Party, 66

V

Vilayat-i-Faqih, 14-39, 59-66

W

White Revolution, 8 ff